FANTASTIC FOOD FOR LESS

LESS WASTE · LESS COST · MORE TASTE

DAIRY COOKBOOK

Contents

Introduction

This book is for everyone who cares about what they eat. Whether you're on a budget or not, if you love good food this book is for you.

It's not about cheap food, it's about cooking fantastic food, more economically and less wastefully. Everything is simple to cook, tastes delicious and won't cost the earth.

The recipes

Each chapter is split into two – *Quick & Easy* and *Take it Easy*. The Quick recipes can be on the table in under half an hour while the Take it Easy recipes take longer to cook, allowing you to put your feet up or get on with something else.

Each recipe in this book uses good quality, *reasonably priced ingredients*.

The recipes have been designed to have *minimal leftovers*. Where they do have any leftovers, they are mostly long-life ingredients, which will keep for several weeks. There are suggestions for leftovers in the *cook's tips* and in the table on page 7 where you can find recipes that share leftover ingredients.

All the dishes have been *triple-tested* to ensure that they work perfectly.

For recipes *suitable for vegetarians* look out for ⓥ. It is assumed that vegetarian cheese or yogurt is used.

Many recipes are *suitable for freezing*; look out for ⓕ.

Large eggs should be used unless otherwise stated. Children and pregnant women should not eat raw or lightly cooked eggs.

The *nutritional information* for each recipe is shown under the title. It also tells you how many each recipe will serve and how long it will take.

Scan the *QR code* under the ingredients list with a smartphone to provide a *handy shopping list*. No internet access is required.

Can we do our bit to save the planet?

**As a nation, every year we throw away around 7 million tonnes of food –
a shocking figure that has serious implications for the environment.**

If we all stopped wasting food that could have been eaten, the benefit to the planet would be the equivalent of taking 1 in 4 cars off the road. It would also mean that we would have an average of £500 more in our pockets to spend on things we love rather than food for the bin.

So how can we change our habits? It's easy, just a few simple steps can make a big difference:

Get organised

Forward planning is essential. Before you shop, plan meals for five days of the week. Check your fridge or freezer first to see what you can make use of. Write these meals down on a notice board or list stuck to the fridge.

When you have eaten all the meals on your list look what is in your fridge or cupboard and make the other two meals from leftovers. Be creative!

Shopping

Try and stick to your list. If you are tempted by multibuy offers make sure you freeze anything that you are unlikely to use before its use-by date. If you often throw away fruit and veg, buy them loose rather than in large packs.

If you have a small household you can buy small portions of meat and fish from the meat/fish counter or from your local butcher/fishmonger. If you want to bulk-buy (which can be more economical) split your pack of meat/fish into portions, wrap well and freeze.

Storage

Place items in your fridge with the shortest shelf-life at the front. Keep fresh food in the packet it came in – some use clever technology to prolong their shelf life. Be freezer-friendly, check use-by dates and anything you are unlikely to use before its date pop in the freezer (check the label and don't freeze if it has already been frozen).

If you cook too much, pop in a freezer-proof tub, label and freeze. Voila, a meal just waiting to be heated up. Place the tub in the fridge overnight to defrost then heat gently on the stove or in the microwave until it is piping hot.

Waste

Think about the foods that often get thrown away.

Bread? Try slicing and freezing it if you use it for toast. Or pop any dry bits into a food processor to make bread crumbs, which freeze really well.

Salads? Don't buy in bags, choose other salad ingredients that come in smaller quantities. Pickle any leftovers.

Vegetables? For soup cook with stock, purée, then freeze.

Herbs? Grow your own outside in summer and on the windowsill in winter.

Cold meat? Buy just a couple of slices from the meat counter.

Sauces? Freeze in small tubs or ice cube trays before they go out of date.

Fruit? For sorbet, cook with sugar and then freeze.

Freezer friendly

Many foods can be frozen and this will significantly prolong their shelf life.

Check the label, freeze by its use-by date, and don't freeze if the label says the item has been previously frozen.

Ensure any cooked foods are completely cool before freezing and always freeze in individual portions. Wrap the food well; store in a plastic tub with a tight-fitting lid or in a well-sealed bag. Squeeze out all the air and label with the date and foodstuff using a permanent pen.

Try eating from the freezer at least once a week so that the carefully frozen food doesn't lie untouched for months!

Ingredients suitable for freezing plus notes

Biscuits
Bought biscuits keep well in an airtight tin but homemade biscuits can be frozen before they're cooked.

Bread
Leave in its original packaging unless it's wrapped in paper, then transfer to a plastic bag.

Butter
Leave in its original packaging.

Cake
Most cakes freeze well but sponge cakes are better frozen before they are filled.

Cheese
Grate hard cheese before freezing and cut soft cheese into portions; don't freeze cottage cheese or Mozzarella.

Chestnuts
Freeze whole in polythene bags.

Chillies
Freeze whole in polythene bags.

Coffee (fresh beans or ground)
Freeze in its vacum-packed bag

Croissants
Freeze in a single layer before sealing in a polythene bag.

Fish
Check it's not been previously frozen, separate into portions, then wrap well.

Fruit
Open freeze raw fruit in a single layer on a tray then pop into a polythene bag; freeze cooked fruit in plastic tubs.

Fruit juice
Freeze in the carton.

Gravy
Freeze in ice cube trays.

Herbs
Freeze whole sprigs in polythene bags; store chopped herbs in small tubs.

Home-cooked meals
Many can be frozen, especially casseroles, curries and bakes, though rice and pasta dishes don't work so well; check recipes for 🄵.

Milk
Freeze in a rigid container.

Meat
Raw or cooked meat freezes well; remove any fat, separate into portions, then wrap well.

Pancakes
Interleave with baking paper, then pop into a polythene bag.

Pastry
Wrap raw pastry well in useful-sized portions.

Pies
Can be frozen raw or cooked, wrapped in polythene bags.

Puddings
Many can be frozen; check recipes for 🄵.

Quiches and tarts
Freeze cooked in polythene bags.

Sauces
Pour into small tubs or ice cube trays.

Soups
Pour into a rigid container.

Vegetables
Peel and chop, blanch in hot water for 2 minutes, then plunge into cold water, drain, dry then freeze.

Yogurt
Freeze in the sealed tub.

Yorkshire Pudding
Freeze in polythene bags.

Recipe leftovers

The recipes in this book have been written to minimise waste. Where they do have leftovers, they are mostly long-life ingredients, which will keep for several weeks.

You will find suggestions for these in some of the cook's tips. In this table you can see which ingredients are leftover and which other recipes they could be used in.

There are a few omissions, namely store cupboard staples (salt and pepper, bread, garlic, butter, milk, stock, oil, flour, sugar or eggs) as they are used in so many recipes. It has been assumed that you buy fruit and vegetables loose in the exact quantity required and that you grow or freeze your own fresh herbs.

Optional ingredients or serving suggestions have not been listed here.

Ingredient	Recipe page no.	Ingredient	Recipe page no.	Ingredient	Recipe page no.
Dried Herbs		Broad beans (frozen)	94	Marshmallows	127
Bay	74, 82, 94, 102, 106	Celery	18, 74	Marzipan	147
Mixed herbs	22, 82	Cheese - Cheddar	9, 10, 11, 14, 15, 22, 26, 45, 49, 61, 62, 65	Mayonnaise	10, 11, 41
Oregano	18, 57, 82			Mustard	9, 10, 11, 26, 49, 50
Sage	13, 42	Cheese - Dbl Gloucester	9, 65, 81		
Thyme	14, 66, 74, 78,	Cheese - Feta	15, 58	Noodles	57, 102
Spices		Cheese - Parmesan	15, 34, 49	Oats/Oatmeal	123, 127, 128, 171
Allspice	85, 93	Cheese - soft	38	Pasta	21, 22, 37, 38, 46, 49, 82, 98
Chilli powder	54, 57, 89	Cheese - Stilton	65, 105		
Coriander seeds	58, 94	Cocoa powder	120, 156, 164	Peas (frozen)	33, 37, 45, 53, 57, 81, 94
Cumin seeds	10, 58, 97	Coffee (instant)	156		
Curry powder	25, 101	Couscous	10	Pesto	9, 12, 34, 70, 98
Dried crushed chillies	38, 74, 77, 106	Cranberry sauce	85		
Ground cinnamon	54, 97, 106, 139, 140	Crème fraîche	15, 29, 70	Pitta bread	10, 29
		Curry paste	69	Rasisins/sultanas	25, 29, 77, 97, 101, 112, 124, 148, 159, 163, 168
Ground coriander	13, 54	Custard powder	116		
Ground cumin	13, 54, 77, 89, 106	Dates/prunes	136, 144		
		Desiccated coconut	139, 167		
Ground ginger	152, 160	Double cream	14, 69	Red wine	42, 61
Ground mixed spice	77, 159, 163	Filo pastry	33	Rice	45, 97
Nutmeg	50, 163	Ginger (root)	54, 69, 77	Single cream	9, 12
Paprika	15, 25, 38, 58, 74, 89, 97	Glacé cherries	136, 155, 168	Soy sauce	53, 57, 102
		Glacé ginger	136	Sweetcorn	33, 53, 74
Turmeric	13, 77, 101	Golden syrup	144, 160, 168	Tomato ketchup	10, 11, 65, 82, 89
		Gravy granules	82		
Other ingredients		Honey	50, 58, 94, 171	Tomato purée	9, 15, 25, 61, 69, 85, 101, 105
Apricots (dried)	29	Horseradish	41, 105		
Bacon	11, 14, 46, 74, 90	Jam/Marmalade	25, 132, 148, 160	Trifle sponges	132
Balsamic vinegar	42			Vanilla extract	120, 144, 167
Banana chips	128	Lemon	9, 10, 11, 25, 33, 34, 37, 124, 163	Wine vinegar	11, 93, 102, 106, 139
Blackcurrant cordial	111			Worcestershire sauce	105
Butternut squash	58	Lentils	13, 101	Yellow split peas	13, 14

Soups & Snacks

Quick & Easy

Garlicky Mushrooms on Toast 9

Toasted Cheese with Ale 9

Black Olive & Tomato Crostini 9

Pesto Toasts 9

Vegetarian Pitta Pizzas 10

Soufflé-Stuffed Tomatoes 10

Sardine Toasts 10

Grilled Mackerel with
Beetroot Couscous 10

Smoked Mackerel & Dill Pâté 11

Hearty Beans on Toast 11

Warm Bacon and Avocado Salad 11

Pigs in Blankets 11

Take it Easy

Roasted Red Pepper Soup 12

Chunky Tomato Soup with
Pesto Croutons 12

Creamy Celery Soup 12

Piquant Parsnip Soup 13

Leek, Parsnip & Potato Soup 13

Spiced Dhal Soup 13

Mushroom & Thyme Soup 14

French Onion Soup 14

Pea & Bacon Soup 14

Potato Salad with Peppers & Brie 15

Beetroot & Feta Baked Potatoes 15

Loaded Potato Skins 15

Baked Stuffed Squash 15

Garlicky Mushrooms on Toast ⓥ

Time 20 mins. Per portion: 287 Kcal,
19g fat (9.9g saturated). Serves 4

Butter 50g (2oz)
Olive oil 1 tbsp
Garlic 4 cloves, peeled and thinly sliced
Mushrooms 450g (1lb), quartered
Bread 4 chunky slices
Lemon juice 1 tbsp
Salt and freshly ground black pepper
Single cream 6 tbsp

Melt the butter with the olive oil in a
large frying pan over a medium heat. Add
the garlic cloves and the mushrooms and
fry quickly, stirring frequently, for about
5 minutes until the mushrooms have
softened.

Meanwhile, toast the bread lightly on
both sides.

Add the lemon juice and seasoning to the
mushrooms and stir for 1 minute. Stir in the
cream and cook for 1 minute until hot.

Pile the mushroom mixture over the toast
on warmed serving plates.

Toasted Cheese with Ale ⓥ

Time 15 mins. Per portion: 590 Kcal,
32g fat (19.2g saturated). Serves 2

Brown ale 150ml (¼ pint)
Double Gloucester cheese 175g (6oz), grated
Mustard 1 tsp
Cornflour 2 tsp, blended in 1 tsp of water
Wholemeal bread 4 thick slices
Salt and freshly ground black pepper

Pour the brown ale into a saucepan over
a low heat and add the Double Gloucester
cheese, mustard and cornflour. Heat gently,
stirring, until the cheese has melted and the
sauce thickens slightly.

Meanwhile, toast the bread. Pour the
warm ale and cheese over the toast (you
might like to grill for a little extra colour at
this stage), season to taste with salt and
pepper, and serve immediately.

Black Olive & Tomato Crostini ⓥ

Time 25 mins. Per portion: 231 Kcal,
16g fat (2.1g saturated). Serves 4

Pitted black olives 165g can, drained
Sunflower oil 4 tbsp
Small French stick 1, cut into thin slices
Garlic 2 cloves, peeled and halved
Tomatoes 2, chopped
Chopped basil or parsley 1 tbsp
Salt and freshly ground black pepper

Preheat the oven to 200°C/400°F/Gas 6.
Put the olives into a food processor and
blend with 2 tablespoons of the oil to a
coarse paste.

Lightly grill the bread slices on both
sides. Rub the garlic cloves over one side of
each slice, put them on a baking sheet and
drizzle with a little of the oil.

Divide the olive mixture between the
bread slices and spread evenly. Top with the
tomatoes and herbs and season well with
salt and pepper.

Bake for 10 minutes until they are piping
hot, then transfer to a serving plate and
serve immediately.

Pesto Toasts ⓥ

Time 15 mins. Per portion: 448 Kcal,
26g fat (15.3g saturated). Serves 4

Bread 8 slices
Pesto 1 tbsp
Tomato purée 4 tsp
Tomatoes 4
Cheddar cheese 275g (10oz)

Lightly toast the bread on both sides, then
spread with the pesto and tomato purée.

Thinly slice the tomatoes and cheese and
arrange on top of the bread.

Grill the toasts for 2–3 minutes until the
cheese is bubbling.

Cut into squares and serve.

Vegetarian Pitta Pizzas ⓥ

Time 25 mins. Per portion: 377 Kcal,
14g fat (8.3g saturated). Serves 2

Pitta breads 2, split in half
Tomato ketchup 8 tsp
Garlic 1 clove, peeled and crushed (optional)
Red or green pepper 1, deseeded and sliced
Mushrooms 75g (3oz), wiped and finely sliced
Salt and freshly ground black pepper
Mozzarella 125g pack, drained and torn
Tomatoes 2, chopped or sliced
Salad to serve (optional)

Preheat the oven to 200°C/400°F/Gas 6.
Put the pitta breads on a baking sheet.
Spread each half with ketchup and add a
little garlic, if using, then divide the pepper
and mushrooms between them.

Season the pizzas and top with chunks of
torn mozzarella, then pieces of tomato.

Cook for 20–23 minutes. Serve two 'pizzas'
per person with a green salad.

Soufflé-Stuffed Tomatoes ⓥ

Time 30 mins. Per portion: 46 Kcal,
3g fat (1.2g saturated). Serves 6

Tomatoes 6
Egg 1, separated
Cheddar cheese 25g (1oz), grated
Mustard ½ tsp
Chopped parsley 2 tsp
Salt and freshly ground black pepper

Preheat the oven to 200°C/400°F/Gas 6.
Cut a slice off the top of each tomato, then
scoop out enough flesh to leave a firm
shell. Reserve the centres to add to soups.

Beat the egg yolk, cheese, mustard and
parsley together in a bowl, then season.

Whisk the egg white in a separate bowl
until stiff. Stir a little egg white into the yolk
mixture to slacken it, then fold in the rest.

Spoon the egg mixture into each tomato
and then place in a small roasting tin,
adding the 'lids' to the base of the tin. Cook
in the oven for 10–12 minutes until risen.

Sardine Toasts

Time 15 mins. Per portion: 237 Kcal,
11g fat (2.1g saturated). Serves 2

Sardines in brine 120g can
Mayonnaise 1 tbsp
Lemon juice 1 tsp
Salt and freshly ground black pepper
Cocktail gherkins 2 (optional), drained and
chopped
Granary bread 2 slices
Tomatoes 2, cut into wedges

Drain the sardines and mash in a bowl
with the mayonnaise, lemon juice and
seasoning. Stir in the gherkins.

Toast the bread on both sides, then spread
one side with the sardine mixture and cut
into triangles. Serve with the tomatoes.

Grilled Mackerel with Beetroot Couscous

Time 25 mins. Per portion: 665 Kcal,
41g fat (7.8g saturated). Serves 4

Mackerel 4, gutted and rinsed
Olive or sunflower oil 3 tbsp
Cumin seeds 3 tsp, roughly crushed
Salt and freshly ground black pepper
Couscous 200g (7oz)
Cooked beetroot in natural juices 225g (8oz),
drained and diced
Orange 1 small, grated zest and juice

Slash each side of the mackerel 3 times.
Place the fish on a grill pan lined with foil.
Drizzle with 2 tbsp oil and 2 tsp cumin
seeds, season and turn to coat with oil.

Preheat the grill to hot and cook for 10–12
minutes, turning once, until browned.

Meanwhile, put the couscous and
beetroot into a heatproof bowl. Add the
remaining cumin and oil, then add the
orange zest and juice and season. Pour over
400ml (14fl oz) boiling water, cover and leave
to stand for 5 minutes.

Fluff up the couscous then spoon it onto
plates. Top each with a cooked mackerel
and spoon over any cooking juices.

Smoked Mackerel & Dill Pâté

Time 10 mins plus chilling. Per portion: 185 Kcal, 8.4g fat (1.3g saturated). Serves 4

Smoked mackerel 225g (8oz), skinned
Chopped dill 3 tbsp
Lemon juice 2 tbsp
Garlic 1 clove, peeled and crushed
Freshly ground black pepper
Double cream 150ml (¼ pint), lightly whipped
Egg white 1, whisked
Lemon wedges to serve (optional)
Melba toast to serve (optional)

Place the mackerel flesh in a bowl. Add the chopped dill, lemon juice, garlic and pepper and mash together well or blend in a food processor.

Fold in the cream and egg white; chill.

Serve with Melba toast and lemon.

Hearty Beans on Toast

Time 15 mins. Per portion: 511 Kcal, 22g fat (7.6g saturated). Serves 2

Baked beans 200g can
Tuna 200g can, drained and flaked
Mayonnaise 2 tbsp
Freshly ground black pepper
Thick slices of bread 4, cut horizontally from a small round loaf
Cheddar cheese 50g (2oz), grated
Tomato 1, sliced

Preheat the grill to hot and gently warm the baked beans in a saucepan. Mix together the tuna and mayonnaise in a bowl, seasoning well with black pepper.

Toast the bread on one side, then turn the slices over and just very lightly toast the other side. Spread the tuna mixture evenly over each slice of toast, going right up to the edges.

Spoon the baked beans over the tuna, sprinkle with the cheese and cook under the grill until the cheese is melted and lightly browned. Add the tomato slices and cook for a further 1 minute before serving.

Warm Bacon and Avocado Salad

Time 25 mins. Per portion: 412 Kcal, 36g fat (8.2g saturated). Serves 4

Olive oil 5 tbsp
Lemon juice or wine vinegar 1 tbsp
Salt and freshly ground black pepper
Streaky bacon 150g (6oz), de-rinded and chopped
Bread 3 slices, diced
Garlic 1 clove, peeled and crushed
Curly leaf lettuce 1, leaves separated and torn
Avocados 2 stoned, peeled and diced

Make the dressing by mixing 3 tbsp of the oil with the lemon juice or vinegar and seasoning in a large bowl.

Dry-fry the bacon until crisp. Keep warm.

Add the remaining oil to the pan, then add the bread and garlic and fry, stirring until browned. Drain and keep warm.

Add the lettuce, avocados, bacon and croutons to the dressing and toss well.

Pigs in Blankets

Time 30 mins. Per portion: 313 Kcal, 23g fat (10.5g saturated). Makes 8

Medium-sliced white bread 8 slices
Butter 110g (4oz)
Tomato ketchup 3 tbsp
Mustard 1 rounded tbsp
Chopped parsley 4 tbsp
Good-quality pork sausages 8, skins removed

Preheat the oven to 200°C/400°F/Gas 6. Remove the crusts from the bread, then use a rolling pin to roll out each slice.

In a saucepan, heat the butter and ketchup together until melted, then stir in the mustard and parsley.

Brush some of the butter mixture over each slice of bread, then place a sausage diagonally across each one. Bring the opposite corners up and over and secure with cocktail sticks. Place on a baking tray, brush with butter and bake for 20–25 minutes until the sausages are cooked.

Roasted Red Pepper Soup V F

Time 55 mins. Per portion: 194 Kcal,
14g fat (7g saturated). Serves 4

Red peppers 4, halved and deseeded
Olive oil 1 tbsp
Butter 50g (2oz)
Onions 2, peeled and chopped
Vegetable stock cubes 2
Salt and freshly ground black pepper
Chopped basil 1–2 tbsp (optional)

Preheat the grill to hot. Spread out the peppers, skin-side up, on a baking sheet and brush with half of the oil. Grill for about 10 minutes, then turn over and brush with oil. Cook for a further 3–5 minutes, until the flesh starts to turn golden.

Place the peppers in a plastic bag. Leave them to cool, then peel off the skins and discard. Roughly chop the pepper flesh.

Melt the butter in a saucepan and fry the onions for 10 minutes until they soften. Add the peppers and cook for 2–3 minutes.

Crumble the stock cubes into the pan and pour in 1 litre (1¾ pints) of water. Bring the mixture to the boil, then reduce the heat, cover and simmer for 20 minutes.

Purée the soup with a hand-held blender, season, and stir in the basil, if using.

Chunky Tomato Soup with Pesto Croutons V F

Time 1 hr. Per portion: 235 Kcal,
13g fat (5.1g saturated). Serves 6

Sunflower oil 2 tbsp
Onions 2, peeled and finely chopped
Potato 1, peeled and finely chopped
Tomatoes 675g (1½lb)
Garlic 2 cloves, peeled and crushed
Plain flour 1 tbsp
Vegetable stock 900ml (1½ pints)
Caster sugar 1 tsp
Salt and freshly ground black pepper
Pesto sauce 4 tsp
Bread 4 thick slices
Butter 50g (2oz)

Heat the oil in a large saucepan, add the onions and potato, cover and fry for 10 minutes, stirring occasionally, until golden.

Meanwhile, cut a cross in the base of each tomato. Put them into a bowl, cover with boiling water and leave for 30 seconds until the skins loosen and burst. Plunge in cold water, then peel away the skin.

Roughly chop the tomatoes and add to the onion with the garlic and cook for 3 minutes. Stir in the flour, vegetable stock, sugar and seasoning.

Bring to the boil, stirring, then reduce the heat, cover and simmer for 25 minutes. Stir in 3 tsp of pesto.

Meanwhile, preheat the grill to hot. Cut the bread into diamond shapes and put on a baking sheet. Beat the butter and 1 tsp pesto together, then spread half of it over one side of each bread shape.

Cook under the grill for 2 minutes until lightly browned. Turn over, spread with pesto and grill.

Serve the soup with hot croutons.

Creamy Celery Soup V F

Time 50 mins. Per portion: 124 Kcal,
11g fat (6.1g saturated). Serves 4–6

Butter 50g (2oz)
Onion 1 large, peeled and chopped
Celery 1 head, about 500g (1lb 2oz), chopped
Vegetable stock 1.25 litres (2 pints)
Salt and freshly ground black pepper
Single cream 4–6 tbsp

Melt the butter in a large saucepan and fry the onion for 5 minutes until softened.

Add the celery and stock and bring to the boil, then reduce the heat, cover and simmer for 25–30 minutes, or until the celery and onions are very soft.

Purée the soup with a hand-held blender, then pass through a sieve. Season to taste, then stir in the cream.

Piquant Parsnip Soup ⓥ ⓕ

Time 1 hr. Per portion: 264 Kcal,
15g fat (7.7g saturated). Serves 4

Butter 25g (1oz)
Parsnips 675g (1½lb), peeled and sliced
Bramley cooking apple 1, peeled and sliced
Vegetable stock 1.25 litres (2 pints)
Dried sage ½ tsp
Single cream 150ml (¼ pint)
Salt and freshly ground black pepper

Melt the butter in a large saucepan over
a medium-low heat and add the parsnips
and apple. Cover and cook gently for 10
minutes, stirring occasionally.

Pour the stock into the saucepan and add
the sage. Bring to the boil, then reduce
the heat, cover and simmer for about 30
minutes until the parsnip is softened.

Purée the soup with a hand-held blender,
and then reheat gently with the cream and
season to taste before serving.

Leek, Parsnip & Potato Soup ⓥ ⓕ

Time 45 mins. Per portion: 249 Kcal,
13g fat (7.3g saturated). Serves 4

Butter 50g (2oz)
Onion 1, peeled and sliced
Parsnips 225g (8oz), peeled and sliced
Leeks 350g (12oz), trimmed and sliced
Potatoes 225g (8oz), peeled and sliced
Vegetable stock 750ml (1¼ pints)
Salt and freshly ground black pepper
Milk 300ml (½ pint)

Melt the butter in a large saucepan over
a medium heat and fry the vegetables for
about 5 minutes.

Add the stock and season. Bring to the
boil, then reduce the heat, cover and
simmer for about 30 minutes until tender.

Purée the soup with a hand-held blender.
Add the milk and reheat gently before
serving in warmed bowls.

Spiced Dhal Soup ⓥ ⓕ

Time 1¼ hrs plus soaking. Per portion: 178 Kcal,
5g fat (0.6g saturated). Serves 8

Yellow split peas 225g (8oz), soaked overnight in
cold water, or **red lentils**
Sunflower oil 2 tbsp
Onions 2, peeled and finely chopped
Parsnips 5, about 350g (12oz), peeled and
chopped
Garlic 4 cloves, peeled and crushed
Ground cumin 1½ tsp
Ground coriander 1½ tsp
Turmeric 2 tsp
Vegetable stock 1.7 litres (3 pints)
Salt and freshly ground black pepper

Drain the soaked peas and set aside.
Heat the oil in a large saucepan over a
medium heat and fry the onions and
parsnips for about 5 minutes until softened
and lightly browned.

Add the garlic and spices and fry for
1minute, stirring. Add the stock and split
peas or lentils and season well with salt and
pepper. Bring the mixture to the boil, then
reduce the heat, cover and simmer for 45
minutes until the peas or lentils are very
soft.

Purée half the soup in a liquidiser or
food processor, then stir it back into the
remaining soup and reheat before serving
in warmed bowls.

Mushroom & Thyme Soup Ⓕ

Time 50 mins. Per portion: 198 Kcal,
10g fat (5.2g saturated). Serves 6

Butter 50g (2oz)
Onions 2, peeled and chopped
Potatoes 450g (1lb), peeled and chopped
Mushrooms 450g (1lb), wiped and chopped
Lemon 1, grated zest and juice
Chicken stock 1.5 litres (2½ pints)
Dried thyme 1 tsp
Salt and freshly ground black pepper
Milk 450ml (¾ pint)

Melt the butter in a large saucepan over a
medium heat and fry the onions for about
5 minutes until softened.

Add the potatoes and mushrooms and fry
for 3–4 minutes, stirring occasionally. Stir
in the lemon zest and juice, stock and the
thyme. Season with salt and pepper.

Bring the mixture to the boil, then reduce
the heat, cover and simmer for 25 minutes

Purée the soup with a hand-held blender,
and then return it to the pan and stir in the
milk. Heat gently before serving.

French Onion Soup Ⓕ

Time 1 hr. Per portion: 230 Kcal,
14g fat (8.1g saturated). Serves 4

Butter 40g (1½oz)
Onions 3, peeled and cut into fine rings
Beef stock 900ml (1½ pints)
Salt and freshly ground black pepper
French bread 4 slices, 2.5cm (1in) thick
Cheddar cheese 50g (2oz), grated

Melt the butter in a large saucepan and
fry the onions for 10–15 minutes until
softened, stirring occasionally.

Pour in the stock and bring to the boil,
then reduce the heat, cover and simmer for
35–40 minutes. Season to taste.

Preheat the grill to hot. Pour the soup into
a flameproof dish and float the bread on
top. Sprinkle with the cheese and then grill
until the cheese has melted.

Pea & Bacon Soup Ⓕ

Time 1½ hrs plus soaking. Per portion: 345 Kcal,
6g fat (1.7g saturated). Serves 6

Dried split peas 500g (1lb 2oz), soaked overnight
in cold water
Rindless streaky bacon 3 rashers, chopped
Onion 1, peeled and chopped
Carrot 1, peeled and diced
Celery 1 stick, chopped
Chicken or ham stock 2.5 litres (4 pints)
Salt and freshly ground black pepper
Double cream 6 tbsp

Drain the soaked peas and set aside.

Put the bacon, onion, carrot and celery in
a large saucepan over a medium heat and
cook for 5–10 minutes until the vegetables
are beginning to soften.

Add the peas and stock and then boil
rapidly, uncovered, for 10 minutes.

Reduce the heat, cover and simmer for
about 1 hour, until the peas are tender.

Purée the soup with a hand-held blender,
season and stir in the cream.

Potato Salad with Peppers & Brie ⓥ

Time 35 mins. Per portion: 292 Kcal, 14g fat (8g saturated). Serves 4

New potatoes 675g (1½lb)
Salt and freshly ground black pepper
Butter 25g (1oz)
Red pepper 1 small, deseeded and sliced
Yellow pepper 1 small, deseeded and sliced
Sun-dried tomato paste 3 tbsp
Lemon 1, juice only
Cherry tomatoes 110g (4oz), halved
Brie 110g (4oz), cut into small cubes

Scrub the potatoes, then put them into a saucepan with just enough lightly salted water to cover them. Cover with a lid and bring the water to the boil. Then reduce the heat and simmer for about 15 minutes until the potatoes are just tender.

Meanwhile, melt the butter in a frying pan over a medium-low heat and fry the peppers for 6–8 minutes until very soft.

Mix together the tomato paste and lemon juice in a large mixing bowl. Drain the cooked potatoes and add to the bowl with the peppers and the buttery pan juices, gently tossing everything together until coated.

When the potatoes have cooled for a few minutes, add the tomatoes and Brie, stirring to mix. Season to taste with salt and pepper, then serve.

Beetroot & Feta Baked Potatoes ⓥ

Time 1½ hrs. Per portion: 250 Kcal, 5g fat (3.2g saturated). Serves 2

Baking potatoes 2
Feta cheese 50g (2oz)
Freshly ground black pepper
Cooked beetroot 150g (5oz), cut into fine strips
Mizuna leaves and/or **lamb's lettuce**

Preheat the oven to 200°C/400°F/Gas 6. Bake the potatoes for 1-1½ hours until cooked through.

Cut a large cross in the top of the cooked potato and squeeze it so that the flesh starts to 'ooze' out.

Crumble the Feta cheese into the top of the potato. Sprinkle with black pepper and then pile the beetroot strips on top. Top with a handful of leaves and serve hot.

Loaded Potato Skins ⓥ

Time 2 hours. Per portion: 325 Kcal, 6g fat (4.7g saturated). Serves 4

Baking potatoes 4
Tomatoes 2, chopped
Garlic and herb soft cheese 200g tub
Cheddar cheese 25g (1oz), grated
Salt and freshly ground black pepper

Preheat the oven to 200°C/400°F/Gas 6. Bake the potatoes for 1-1½ hours until cooked through.

Cut each potato in half and then scoop out the flesh, keeping the skins intact.

In a bowl, mix the potato with the tomatoes, soft cheese and Cheddar and season well. Pile the potato mixture back into the skins and bake for 15-20 minutes.

Baked Stuffed Squash ⓥ

Time 1 hr. Per portion: 231 Kcal, 7g fat (3.6g saturated). Serves 2

Butternut squash 1, halved and deseeded
Crème fraîche 3 tbsp
Paprika 1½ tsp
Spring onions 3, trimmed and sliced
Grated Parmesan-like hard cheese 2 tbsp
Breadcrumbs 2 tbsp

Preheat the oven to 200°C/400°F/Gas 6. Place the squash halves on a baking sheet and roast for 40-45 minutes until soft.

Scoop out the flesh, mash with a fork and then mix with the crème fraîche, 1 tsp paprika and the onions. Pile back into the skins, sprinkle with the cheese, breadcrumbs and remaining paprika and bake for 10-15 minutes until browned.

Main Courses
Quick & Easy

Main Courses
Take it Easy

Cashew & Vegetable Stir-Fry

(V)

Time 15 minutes.   Per portion: 463 Kcal, 40g fat (17.4g saturated)

Serves 4

Butter 25g (1oz)

Garlic 2 cloves, peeled and crushed

Carrots 3, peeled and thinly sliced

Peppers 2, any colour, deseeded and sliced

Celery sticks 4, sliced

Mushrooms 175g (6oz), wiped and sliced

Spring onions 8, trimmed and sliced

Cashew nuts 110g (4oz), toasted

Dried oregano 1 tsp

Double cream 150ml pot

Salt and freshly ground black pepper

Cooked noodles to serve (optional)

Scan the **QR Code** with a smartphone for an ingredients shopping list

Melt the butter in a large frying pan or wok over a medium heat and stir-fry the garlic and carrots for 3 minutes. Add all the remaining vegetables and stir-fry for 1–2 minutes, stirring constantly. Stir in the nuts, transfer to a plate and keep warm.

Add the oregano and cream to the pan and heat until the sauce is hot but not boiling. Season to taste.

Serve the stir-fried vegetables on a bed of noodles, if you like, with the sauce poured over the top.

Cook's tips

Toast the cashew nuts by dry-frying for a few minutes. To spice it up, fry some grated fresh ginger with the garlic. You could also turn up the heat with a chopped chilli.

This colourful dish is quick to prepare.
The combination of crunchy veg and nuts works
beautifully with the velvety texture of the cream.

Comforting and delicious, with a decadently creamy
sauce, this recipe is perfect for a weekday dinner
using whatever veg you have left in your fridge.

Garlicky Green Vegetable Pasta

V

Time 15 minutes. Per portion: 450 Kcal, 16g fat (9.6g saturated)

Serves 4

Dried tagliatelle 300g (11oz)

Fine green beans 110g (4oz), trimmed and halved

Broccoli 110g (4oz), broken into small florets

Butter 25g (1oz)

Courgette 1 large, diced

Soft cheese with garlic and herbs 250g tub

Milk 4 tbsp

Salt and freshly ground black pepper

Toasted pine nuts 25g (1oz) (optional)

Scan the **QR Code** with a smartphone for an ingredients shopping list

Bring a large saucepan of lightly salted water to the boil and cook the tagliatelle according to the packet's instructions. Add the green beans and broccoli during the last 5 minutes of cooking. Drain well and return to the pan.

Meanwhile, melt the butter in a frying pan over a medium-low heat and fry the courgette for 4–5 minutes until just softened. Add the soft cheese and milk to the pan and gently stir in until it melts. Season to taste.

To serve, toss the pasta with the creamy sauce and pile into warmed serving bowls. Sprinkle each portion with pine nuts, if using.

Cook's tip

You can easily substitute the vegetables for others that you have leftover in the fridge, or for frozen vegetables.

Mediterranean Pasta Bake

Time 30 minutes. Per portion: 611 Kcal, 36g fat (20.2g saturated)

Serves 4

Pasta shapes 175g (6oz)

Butter 50g (2oz)

Red onion 1, peeled and sliced

Garlic 1 clove, peeled and crushed

Button mushrooms 150g (5oz), wiped and halved

Courgette 1, cut into batons

Baby corn 110g (4oz), halved

Tomato pasta sauce 1 x 340/350g jar

Eggs 2

Greek-style plain yogurt 300g (11oz)

Mature Cheddar cheese 150g (5oz), grated

Dried mixed herbs 1 tsp

Salt and freshly ground black pepper

Preheat the oven to 200°C/400°F/Gas 6. Bring a large saucepan of lightly salted water to the boil and cook the pasta according to the packet's instructions.

Meanwhile, melt the butter in a large frying pan over a medium heat and fry the onion and garlic for about 5 minutes until softened. Add all the remaining vegetables and cook for 5 minutes, stirring frequently.

Drain the pasta well and add to the vegetable mixture with the pasta sauce, stirring to combine. Transfer to a large buttered ovenproof dish.

Beat together the eggs and yogurt, then stir in the cheese. Add the herbs and season with salt and pepper. Pour evenly over the pasta and vegetables, then bake for 20 minutes until set and golden brown. Serve at once.

Scan the **QR Code** with a smartphone for an ingredients shopping list

Cook's tips

You can use any type of tomato-based pasta sauce – choose which is best value; tomato & basil and tomato & red pepper work particularly well. You could use other regional British cheeses in this pasta bake as a change from Cheddar – try Red Leicester or Double Gloucester instead.

The moussaka- like topping on this dish is
its pièce de résistance, turning an ordinary
pasta dish into a delicious delight.

This mildly spiced curry turns ordinary
vegetables into a truly scrummy meal.
Who needs meat when you can eat like this?

Cauliflower & Potato Curry

Ⓥ Ⓕ

Time 30 minutes. Per portion: 267 Kcal, 6g fat (1.2g saturated)

Serves 4

Olive oil 1 tbsp

Onion 1, peeled and chopped

Curry powder 1 tbsp

Paprika 1 tsp

Tomato purée 2 tsp

Lemon juice 2 tsp

Apricot jam or redcurrant jelly
1 tbsp

Semi-skimmed milk
300ml (½ pint)

Raisins or sultanas 50g (2oz)

Carrots 400g (14oz),
peeled and sliced

Cauliflower 400g (14oz),
broken into florets

Potatoes 400g (14oz),
peeled and cubed

Warm naan bread to serve
(optional)

Scan the **QR Code** with
a smartphone for an
ingredients shopping list

Add the olive oil to a large pan and fry the chopped onion gently for a few minutes, without browning. Add the curry powder and paprika and cook for a further 2–3 minutes.

Add the tomato purée, lemon juice, jam or jelly, milk and raisins or sultanas. Bring to the boil and then simmer, uncovered, for 10 minutes.

Meanwhile, cook the vegetables in a pan of boiling water for 5–10 minutes, as required.

Drain the vegetables well and stir into the curry sauce. Serve with naan bread and raita if you like (see cook's tip).

Cook's tip

If you want to serve with raita, simply mix some chopped
mint and cucumber with low fat natural yogurt.

Mushroom Pancakes

V

Time 30 minutes. Per portion: 413 Kcal, 26g fat (12.7g saturated)

Serves 4

Plain flour 110g (4oz) plus 2 tbsp

Egg 1

Milk 700ml (1 pint 4fl oz)

Vegetable oil for brushing

Butter 75g (3oz)

Mushrooms 450g (1lb) button or mixed, wiped and sliced

Mustard ½ tsp

Chopped parsley 2 tbsp

Salt and freshly ground black pepper

Cheddar cheese 50g (2oz) (optional)

Green salad to serve (optional)

Scan the **QR Code** with a smartphone for an ingredients shopping list

To make the pancakes, sift 110g (4oz) of flour into a bowl and break in the egg. Gradually add 125ml (4fl oz) milk, beating to form a smooth batter. Pour in another 125ml (4fl oz) milk and beat until smooth.

Brush a non-stick frying pan with oil and pour in enough of the pancake batter to coat the base. Cook until the pancake moves freely, turn and cook until golden. Repeat until you have 8 pancakes. Keep warm.

Melt 50g (2oz) of the butter in a deep frying pan over a medium heat and fry the mushrooms for 4–5 minutes, until softened and starting to brown. Remove from the pan and keep warm.

Melt the remaining butter in the pan and add the 2 tbsp flour. Cook for 1–2 minutes, then gradually add the remaining milk, beating well and allowing the mixture to come to the boil between each addition of milk. Simmer the sauce gently for 2 minutes, then stir in the mustard, parsley, mushrooms and seasoning.

Preheat the grill to hot. Divide the mushroom mixture between the pancakes, and fold or roll each one up. Place them on a buttered dish, sprinkle with cheese if you like and then place under the grill until the cheese melts and turns golden. Serve immediately with a green salad, if using.

Cook's tips

If you have any bacon in the fridge, chop up a few rashers, fry them and add to the mushrooms. You could use tarragon in place of the parsley.

Extend Pancake Day further than
Shrove Tuesday and cook these scrummy
pancakes whenever you fancy.

Surprisingly filling, this Egyptian-inspired dish is so quick and easy to prepare it makes a healthy weekday dinner.

Falafel Pittas
with Fruity Crunchy Salad

V

Time 20 minutes. Per portion: 554 Kcal, 24g fat (3.2g saturated)

Serves 2

Falafel about 200g (7oz)

Pitta bread 2

Crème fraîche 3 tbsp

Milk 1 tbsp

Salt and freshly ground black pepper

Red or white cabbage 50g (2oz), shredded

Dessert apple 1 small, peeled and chopped

Ready-to-eat dried apricots 25g (1oz), chopped

Raisins 15g (½oz)

Little gem lettuce 1, shredded

Tomato 1, sliced

Scan the **QR Code** with a smartphone for an ingredients shopping list

Preheat the oven and warm the falafel according to the packet's instructions. Place the pitta bread in the oven during the last 3 minutes of cooking.

Meanwhile, make the salad. In a medium-sized bowl whisk together the crème fraîche and milk and season to taste with salt and pepper. Add the cabbage, apple, apricots and raisins and mix well.

Split open each pitta and fill with the lettuce and tomato and some of the fruity salad, then top with the falafel. Serve with the remaining fruity salad.

Cook's tips

Make the salad quickly by popping the ingredients into a food processor and pulsing it a few times – add the cabbage first, then add any leftover dried fruit. Use any leftover crème fraîche to make a dip for crudités by mixing with herbs and grated cheese.

Fish Provençal

Time 20 minutes. Per portion: 323 Kcal, 15g fat (2.2g saturated)

Serves 2

Olive oil 2 tbsp

Onion 1 large, peeled and chopped

Garlic 2 cloves, peeled and crushed

Chopped tomatoes 400g can, drained

Olives 50g (2oz), pitted

Thyme 2 tbsp

Salt and freshly ground black pepper

Cod, coley or haddock steaks 2 x 150g (5oz)

Cooked new potatoes and rocket to serve (optional)

Scan the **QR Code** with a smartphone for an ingredients shopping list

Add the oil to a large non-stick frying pan and gently fry the onion for 5 minutes, until soft. Add the garlic, tomatoes, olives and thyme and bring to the boil. Season well and simmer for 4 minutes.

Make a gap in the sauce and set the fish fillets, skin-side down on the base of the frying pan. Cook for a further 4 minutes and then turn over and cook for 2 minutes more or until cooked through.

Spoon the sauce over the fish and serve with new potatoes and rocket, if you like.

Cook's tips

For a little more kick, you can buy chopped tomatoes with chilli. You could also add a few capers if you like. Buy any white fish that is on offer – tilapia fillets can work beautifully in this dish.

The Med on a plate – colourful,
flavourful, simple and quick.
What more could you want?

This recipe is a tasty, quick and easy alternative to conventional fish pie. It's really versatile – just choose whichever white fish is on offer at the fish counter.

Smoked Fish Filo Bake

Time 30 minutes. Per portion: 439 Kcal, 16g fat (9.4g saturated)

Serves 4

Butter 60g (2½oz), melted

Plain flour 40g (1½oz)

Milk 450ml (¾ pint)

Smoked haddock 450g (1lb), skinned and cubed

Frozen peas 75g (3oz)

Sweetcorn kernels ½ x 198g can, drained

Salt and freshly ground black pepper

Chopped parsley 1 tbsp

Lemon ½, grated zest and juice

Filo pastry 4 sheets

Sesame seeds 2 tbsp (optional)

Scan the **QR Code** with a smartphone for an ingredients shopping list

Preheat the oven to 190°C/375°F/ Gas 5. Melt 40g (1½oz) of the butter in a saucepan, add the flour and beat to form a paste. Gradually add the milk, bringing the mixture to the boil between each addition of liquid. Once all the milk has been added, simmer the white sauce gently for 2–3 minutes to ensure the flour is cooked through.

Add the haddock, peas and sweetcorn to the sauce and cook for 5 minutes. Season with salt and pepper and add the parsley and lemon zest and juice. Transfer to a shallow, ovenproof dish.

Divide each sheet of filo pastry into three and brush one side with melted butter. Scrunch up the pastry and lay on top of the fish mixture. Sprinkle with the sesame seeds, if using, and bake for about 20 minutes until golden.

Cook's tips

Keep the filo pastry well wrapped when you're not handling it as it dries out very quickly. Use any leftovers to make little sweet parcels filled with mincemeat. Leftover sweetcorn can be mixed with tuna and mayonnaise for a sandwich filling or baked potato topping.

Pesto Crusted Salmon

Time 25 minutes. Per portion: 403 Kcal, 25g fat (7.8g saturated)

Serves 4

Fresh white breadcrumbs
50g (2oz)

Grated Parmesan cheese
2 tbsp

Butter 25g (1oz), softened

Salt and freshly ground black pepper

Lemon 1, grated zest only

Pesto 2 tbsp

Salmon fillets 4, each about 150g (5oz)

Cooked new potatoes and peas to serve (optional)

Scan the **QR Code** with a smartphone for an ingredients shopping list

Preheat the oven to 200°C/400°F/Gas 6. Mix together the breadcrumbs, cheese, butter, seasoning, lemon zest and pesto.

Place the salmon fillets on a sheet of baking parchment on a baking tray.

Divide the topping between the salmon fillets, pressing it down so that it stays on the salmon while it's cooking.

Bake in the centre of the oven for 12–15 minutes, until the breadcrumb topping is a golden colour and the salmon is just cooked. Take care not to overcook the salmon or it will become dry – if white juices start to come out, then it's overcooked. Serve at once with new potatoes and peas, if using.

Cook's tips

Salmon fillets can be expensive, so look out for multibuy offers and pop any you don't need in the freezer. If you don't have pesto, try this recipe with sun-dried tomato paste or leftover pasta sauce instead.

Leftover pesto? Here's the perfect recipe and it's so speedy you will only have to spend a few minutes doing the prep.

This is a deliciously light and fresh dish that's whipped up in no time. The salmon adds a decadent touch.

Salmon, Lemon & Asparagus Pasta

Time 20 minutes. Per portion: 655 Kcal, 35g fat (20.8g saturated)

Serves 4

Tagliatelle 300g (11oz)

Asparagus tips 100/125g pack, halved

Butter 25g (1oz)

Frozen peas 150g (5oz)

Crème fraîche 250ml pot

Milk 4 tbsp

Lemon 1, grated zest only

Salt and freshly ground black pepper

Ready-cooked lemon and herb salmon 185g packet, flaked

Scan the **QR Code** with
a smartphone for an
ingredients shopping list

Bring a saucepan of lightly salted water to the boil, add the tagliatelle and cook for about 10–12 minutes, or according to packet's instructions, until just tender. Add the asparagus tips during the last 4 minutes, then drain well.

Meanwhile, melt the butter in a saucepan and add the peas, then stir in the crème fraîche, milk and lemon zest (reserving a little for garnish). Heat gently, stirring, for about 3 minutes, then season to taste.

Drain the pasta, then return it to the saucepan and add the sauce, stirring gently to mix. Divide between 4 warmed bowls. Scatter with the salmon flakes and lemon zest and serve at once.

Cook's tip

Use unwaxed lemons if possible, otherwise just scrub ordinary ones thoroughly before grating the zest. Remember to use only the yellow part – the white pith has a bitter flavour and will spoil the taste of the dish.

Tuna Arrabiata

Time 25 minutes. Per portion: 399 Kcal, 4g fat (0.6g saturated)

Serves 4

Sunflower oil 1 tbsp

Onion 1, peeled and finely chopped

Closed cup mushrooms 110g (4oz), sliced

Garlic 2 cloves, peeled and finely chopped

Mild smoked paprika 1 tsp

Dried crushed chillies a large pinch–¼ tsp, to taste

Chopped tomatoes 400g can

Fish or vegetable stock 250ml (8fl oz)

Salt and freshly ground black pepper

Dried tagliatelle 350g (12oz)

Soft cheese 110g (4oz) (optional)

Tuna chunks in spring water 200g can, drained

Chopped parsley to garnish (optional)

Scan the **QR Code** with a smartphone for an ingredients shopping list

Heat the oil in a saucepan over a medium heat and fry the onion for about 5 minutes until softened and lightly browned.

Stir in the mushrooms and cook for a few minutes until just beginning to colour, then mix in the garlic, paprika and crushed chillies. Cook briefly then mix in the tomatoes, stock and plenty of seasoning and reduce the heat. Let the sauce simmer, uncovered, for 10 minutes, stirring from time to time until thickened.

Meanwhile, bring a large saucepan of lightly salted water to the boil, add the tagliatelle and cook according to the packet's instructions, until just tender.

Drain the pasta into a colander and return to the dried pan. Add the tomato sauce and soft cheese, if using, to the pasta and stir together until the cheese has just melted. Add the tuna and mix lightly so that the fish doesn't break up too much. Serve sprinkled with parsley, if using.

Cook's tips

The sauce is given a creamy luxurious finish with soft cheese. An unopened pack keeps for ages in the fridge and can be used to top baked potatoes with chopped ham or flaked tuna and served with a salad; mix with icing sugar as a filling or frosting for cakes, or spread on toast as a change to butter.

This dish is packed full of flavour and is
a handy store cupboard standby for those
nights when you haven't had time to shop.

Forget fish and chips, which is now a pretty expensive indulgence. Instead, enjoy these fish cakes with chunky homemade potato wedges.

Mackerel Fish Cakes

Ⓕ

Time 20 minutes. Per portion: 681 Kcal, 52g fat (12.4g saturated)

Serves 4

Peppered smoked mackerel fillets 345g pack

Mashed potato 350g (12oz)

Chopped parsley 1 tbsp

Creamed horseradish 2–3 tbsp

Salt and freshly ground black pepper

Egg 1, lightly beaten

Milk 2 tbsp

Fresh white breadcrumbs 75g (3oz)

Butter 25g (1oz)

Sunflower oil 1 tbsp

Mayonnaise 4 tbsp

Baked potato wedges and salad to serve (optional)

Scan the **QR Code** with a smartphone for an ingredients shopping list

Flake the mackerel fillets and stir into the mashed potato, along with the parsley, 1 tablespoon of horseradish sauce and seasoning.

Divide the mixture into 8 and mould each portion into shape. Beat the egg with the milk, dip the fish cakes in the egg mixture and then coat in breadcrumbs.

Heat the butter and oil in a large frying pan over a medium heat until foaming and cook the fish cakes for 4–5 minutes on each side (in batches, if necessary) until they are golden brown and warmed through.

Stir the remaining horseradish into the mayonnaise and season to taste with salt and pepper.

Serve the fish cakes with the flavoured mayonnaise, and with potato wedges and salad, if you like.

Cook's tips

If your pack of mackerel is smaller than 345g, add two chopped hardboiled eggs with the parsley. When making mash, cook a huge batch and freeze in portions. For speedy wedges, microwave baking potatoes for 5 minutes. Cut into wedges, coat in olive oil and bake in the oven until cooked through.

Liver with Balsamic Glazed Shallots

Time 20 minutes. Per portion: 288 Kcal, 16g fat (7.8g saturated)

Serves 4

Olive or sunflower oil 1 tbsp

Shallots 350g (12oz), peeled, halved if large

Light muscovado (or granulated) sugar 4 tsp

Balsamic vinegar 2 tbsp

Frozen chicken livers 500g (1lb 2oz), defrosted

Butter 50g (2oz)

Fresh sage leaves small bunch or 1 tsp dried

Closed cup mushrooms 150g (5oz), wiped and sliced

Sherry, red wine or chicken stock 4 tbsp

Salt and freshly ground black pepper

Mash and steamed cabbage to serve (optional)

Heat the oil in a large frying pan over a medium heat and stir-fry the shallots for about 5 minutes until just beginning to soften. Sprinkle with the sugar, add the vinegar and fry for another 5 minutes, turning frequently until caramelised.

Put the chicken livers in a sieve, rinse with cold water then drain well. Tip out on to a chopping board and cut into large chunks, discarding any white cores. Add the butter and sage to the frying pan and when the butter has melted add the livers and mushrooms and fry for 3–4 minutes until the livers are browned but still slightly pink inside.

Stir in the sherry, wine or stock, season lightly with salt and pepper and cook for 1 minute then serve with mashed potato and steamed green cabbage, if using.

Scan the **QR Code** with a smartphone for an ingredients shopping list

Cook's tips

Chicken livers are so cheap and are packed with iron and protein. The secret is to cook them quickly until still slightly pink in the centre. They can also be fried with butter, garlic and mushrooms and tossed with tagliatelle. Or, make as above, adding 2 cloves garlic, then purée and chill until set and serve as pâté.

Forget about cardboard-like liver and
bacon from school days, this tasty version
will win round the sceptics.

Here you have a scrumptiously 'soupy'
risotto using staple ingredients for
an easy everyday meal.

Cheddar Cheese Risotto with Bacon

Time 30 minutes. Per portion: 478 Kcal, 23g fat (12g saturated)

Serves 4

Butter 25g (1oz)

Risotto rIce 225g (8oz)

Spring onions 8, trimmed and chopped

Hot vegetable stock 900ml (1½ pints)

Smoked streaky bacon 8 rashers, de-rinded and halved

Frozen peas 200g (7oz)

Freshly ground black pepper

Mature Cheddar cheese 110g (4oz), diced

Scan the **QR Code** with a smartphone for an ingredients shopping list

Melt the butter in a large non-stick saucepan and add the rice, coating it well in the butter. Stir in the spring onions and about 150ml (¼ pint) of the stock and simmer until almost absorbed. Pour in more stock, a ladleful at a time and each time waiting for the liquid to be almost absorbed before adding more, simmering until the rice is almost cooked. The mixture should not be dry.

Meanwhile, grill the bacon rashers until crisp.

Add the peas and season well with pepper. Heat through, then stir in the Cheddar cheese. When the cheese starts to melt, serve with the bacon rashers piled on top.

Cook's tip
Risotto is a really simple dish to perfect at home – its success depends on patience though; take your time adding the stock and you will reap the rewards.

Nutty Bacon Pasta

Time 25 minutes. Per portion: 738 Kcal, 36g fat (10.8g saturated)

Serves 4

Penne pasta 350g (12oz)

Tomatoes 8, halved

Olive oil 4 tbsp

Light muscovado sugar 1 tbsp

Salt and freshly ground black pepper

Butter 50g (2oz)

Smoked bacon bits 110g (4oz)

Roughly chopped walnuts 50g (2oz)

Fresh white breadcrumbs 50g (2oz)

Garlic 1 clove, peeled and crushed

Chopped basil 2 tbsp (optional)

Scan the **QR Code** with a smartphone for an ingredients shopping list

Bring a saucepan of lightly salted water to the boil, add the pasta and cook for 10–12 minutes, or as directed on the packet.

Meanwhile, preheat the grill to hot. Place the tomato halves on a grill pan, cut side up, brush with 2 tablespoons of the olive oil, sprinkle with the sugar and season with salt and pepper. Cook under the grill for 5–8 minutes, or until the tomatoes start to char, then remove from the grill and keep warm until the pasta is cooked.

Melt half the butter in a frying pan over a medium heat and cook the bacon bits for 5–7 minutes until they start to crisp, then remove them from the pan.

Add the remaining butter to the pan, tip in the walnuts, breadcrumbs and garlic, and cook until the breadcrumbs turn golden. Remove the pan from the heat and stir in the basil (if using) and bacon bits and then season to taste.

When the pasta is cooked, drain and return it to the pan. Pour the remaining oil over the pasta and stir in the tomatoes and the walnut mixture. Serve immediately sprinkled with more basil, if using.

Cook's tip

For a vegetarian version, leave out the bacon bits and stir in a few rocket or baby spinach leaves at the end of cooking so they wilt into the pasta.

With a few simple ingredients you can quickly
knock up the most delicious – and cheap – dish
that also has plenty of texture and flavour.

Wholesome and comforting, this dish makes a
delicious family meal – while hiding the vegetables
from those who are less keen on them.

Hearty Macaroni Cheese

Time 30 minutes. Per portion: 423 Kcal, 13g fat (7g saturated)

Serves 4

Macaroni 250g (9oz)

Leek 1, washed, trimmed and thickly sliced

Broccoli 110g (4oz), cut into equal-sized florets

Streaky bacon 4 rashers (optional)

Semi-skimmed milk 350ml (12fl oz)

Plain flour 3 tbsp

English mustard 1 tsp

Extra-mature Cheddar cheese 110g (4oz), grated

Salt and freshly ground black pepper

Tomatoes 2, cut into wedges

Grated Parmesan cheese 2 tbsp, (optional)

Scan the **QR Code** with a smartphone for an ingredients shopping list

Bring a large saucepan of lightly salted water to the boil, add the macaroni and cook for 5 minutes. Then add the leek and broccoli and cook for 5 minutes.

Meanwhile, preheat the grill to hot and cook the streaky bacon rashers, if using. Pour the milk into a saucepan and, over a medium heat, whisk in the flour. Bring to the boil and keep whisking to make a smooth sauce. Simmer for 4 minutes and then add the mustard and half the Cheddar and season to taste with salt and pepper.

Put a flameproof dish under the grill to heat up. Drain the pasta and vegetables well. Tip them back into the saucepan and gently stir in the cheese sauce. Spoon the mixture into the hot dish and sprinkle with the rest of the Cheddar.

Arrange the tomato wedges on top and snip the bacon, if using, with scissors, into small pieces, and tuck them into the sauce. Sprinkle with Parmesan, or more Cheddar if you prefer, and put the dish under the grill to brown the top.

Cook's tips

Try this dish with other vegetables – use up any leftovers and different varieties of cheese. It's fun to experiment with different flavour combinations. If you are cooking for children, you may want to chop the vegetables into small pieces.

Honey Mustard Sausages with Colcannon

(F)

Time 30 minutes. Per portion: 492 Kcal, 29g fat (13.3g saturated)

Serves 4

Potatoes 680g (1lb 8oz), peeled and cut into chunks

Leek 1, trimmed and finely sliced

Savoy cabbage 225g (8oz), finely shredded

Butter 50g (2oz)

Chipolata sausages 12

Milk 6 tbsp

Salt and freshly ground black pepper

Grated nutmeg a pinch

Coarse-grain mustard 1 tbsp

Honey 1 tbsp

Scan the **QR Code** with a smartphone for an ingredients shopping list

Put the potatoes into a saucepan with just enough lightly salted water to cover them. Cover with the lid and bring the water to the boil. Then reduce the heat and simmer for about 15 minutes until the potatoes are tender. Steam the leek and cabbage over the potatoes for the last 5-6 minutes of cooking.

Meanwhile, melt a knob of the butter in a frying pan over a medium heat and cook the sausages, turning them occasionally, for about 10 minutes, until browned all over and almost cooked through.

Drain the potatoes, reserving 6 tbsp of the cooking water. Put the potatoes back in the pan and dry over a low heat for 30 seconds or so. Add the milk, bring it to the boil, take off the heat and add the rest of the butter. Season well with salt and pepper and mash until smooth. Drain the greens well and stir them into the mash with a good sprinkling of nutmeg, to taste.

Drain almost all the fat from the frying pan if necessary. Mix the mustard and honey in a small bowl, then spoon it over the sausages with the reserved cooking water and cook for another minute or so, turning them, until they are cooked through and have a sticky glaze. Serve the mash with the sausages piled on top and drizzled with any extra sticky glaze.

Cook's tips

For fluffy mash you need floury potatoes, so look out for Maris Piper, King Edward and Desiree, or good all-rounders Estima. Instead of the cabbage and leek you could use carrot, swede or turnip: simply add to the cooking water with the potatoes.

If it's comfort food you're after, you can't go far wrong with this updated version of an Irish classic.

Rich, colourful and flavourful, this
storecupboard standby is something
you'll cook again and again.

Chorizo Fried Rice

Time 15 minutes. Per portion: 476 Kcal, 24g fat (11g saturated)

Serves 2

Butter 15g (½oz)

Garlic 1 clove, peeled and crushed

Mushrooms 50g (2oz), wiped and sliced

Microwave basmati rice 250g packet

Chorizo 75g (3oz), chopped

Egg 1, beaten

Frozen peas 75g (3oz)

Frozen sweetcorn 75g (3oz)

Soy sauce 1–2 tbsp

Scan the **QR Code** with a smartphone for an ingredients shopping list

Melt the butter in a wok or frying pan over a medium heat and sauté the garlic and mushrooms for 5 minutes. Set aside.

Meanwhile, cook the rice in the microwave according to the packet's instructions.

Add the chorizo and egg to the pan and cook until lightly scrambled.

Add the peas and sweetcorn and cook for 2 minutes and then add the rice and mushrooms and cook for a further 2 minutes until everything is hot.

Serve on warmed plates sprinkled with soy sauce.

Cook's tips

You could replace the mushrooms with peppers, if you prefer. For an even more cost-effective meal you could cook your own basmati rice rather than using the microwave version. It will just take a little longer to prepare.

Aromatic Lamb Burgers

F

Time 15 minutes. Per portion: 273 Kcal, 18g fat (6.8g saturated)

Serves 4

Shallot or small onion 1, peeled and finely chopped

Garlic 1 clove, peeled and finely chopped

Grated root ginger 1 tbsp

Chopped coriander 4 tbsp

Ground cumin ½ tsp

Ground coriander ½ tsp

Ground cinnamon ½ tsp

Mild chilli powder ½ tsp

Minced lamb 500g (1lb 2oz)

Sunflower oil 2 tbsp

Salt and freshly ground black pepper

Toasted ciabatta, red onion, rocket and sweet chilli sauce to serve (optional)

Scan the **QR Code** with a smartphone for an ingredients shopping list

Mix the shallot or onion, garlic, ginger, herbs and spices in a large bowl. Add the lamb and scrunch it all together with your hands until it is evenly mixed.

Divide the mixture into eight portions and lightly shape each one into a round and then flatten with your hand to make burgers about 8cm (3¼in) in diameter. Chill for 30 minutes if you have time.

Heat a large frying pan over a medium heat, lightly oil the burgers and season with salt and pepper. Cook the burgers for 2–3 minutes, pressing them down lightly in the pan with a spatula. Turn them over and cook for another 2–3 minutes, or 5 minutes if you prefer them to be well-done.

Serve the burgers on toasted ciabatta with onion slices, rocket and a sweet chilli sauce, if using.

Cook's tip

If you can, make the burgers the day before you intend to cook them because then the spices have more time to blend into the meat. Double wrap them in cling film to prevent the garlic and spice infiltrating the more sensitive dairy items in your fridge.

Enjoy a change from run-of-the-mill
beef burgers with these spicy
succulent lamb patties.

This surprising combination of flavours works
wonderfully well together. It may not seem like a huge
quantity of beef but it still provides a filling dish.

Chilli Beef Noodles

Time 15 minutes. Per portion: 494Kcal, 15g fat (4.4g saturated)

Serves 3

Egg noodles 2 nests

Olive oil 1 tbsp

Beef frying steak 175g (6oz), thinly sliced

Red onion 1, peeled and cut into 8 wedges

Frozen peas 110g (4oz)

Ready prepared stir-fry vegetables 225g pack

Chilli powder ½ tsp

Dried oregano ½ tsp

Sherry 2 tbsp (optional)

Soy sauce 2 tbsp

Scan the **QR Code** with a smartphone for an ingredients shopping list

Cook the noodles according to the packet's instructions.

Meanwhile, heat the oil in a large frying pan or wok and fry the beef and onion for 4-5 minutes, stirring occasionally, until browned all over. Remove from the pan and keep warm.

Add the peas and stir-fry vegetables to the pan and cook for 2-3 minutes. Then stir in all the remaining ingredients with 4 tbsp water. Stir in the beef and drained noodles and cook for 1 minute before serving.

Cook's tips

Ready prepared stir-fry vegetables are really inexpensive to buy and make midweek cooking super-speedy. If you don't have sherry available then replace it and the water with 6 tbsp beef stock.

Autumn Vegetables with Feta

(V)

Time 50 minutes. Per portion: 454 Kcal, 23g fat (8g saturated)

Serves 4

Butternut squash 450g (1lb), about ½ the squash

Sweet potato 450g (1lb)

Parsnips 450g (1lb)

Cumin seeds 1 tsp

Coriander seeds 2 tsp

Paprika 1 tsp

Olive or sunflower oil 4 tbsp

Salt and freshly ground black pepper

Runny honey 1 tbsp

Feta cheese 200g (7oz)

Chopped mint 2 tbsp to serve (optional)

Warmed pitta bread to serve (optional)

Scan the **QR Code** with a smartphone for an ingredients shopping list

Preheat the oven to 200°C/400°F/Gas 6. Cut the squash in half, scoop out the seeds and then peel away the skin. Peel the sweet potato and parsnips, then cut all the vegetables into similar-sized chunks.

Crush the cumin and coriander seeds in a pestle and mortar or improvise using a mug and the end of a rolling pin. Add the seeds and paprika to a large plastic bag with the oil and a generous amount of salt and pepper. Squeeze the bag to mix, then add the vegetables and shake.

Preheat a large roasting tin in the oven for 5 minutes, then tip the vegetables out of the bag into the tin and spread into an even layer. Roast the vegetables for 30 minutes, turning once.

Turn the vegetables again and drizzle with the honey. Roast for 5–10 more minutes until browned around the edges. Crumble Feta over the top and scatter with mint, if using. Serve with warmed pitta if you like.

Cook's tips

The beauty of this dish is that you can use whatever root vegetables you have available. Chop the leftover squash and use for soup: fry an onion, add the squash and 1 tbsp curry paste. Cook for 1 minute then cover with vegetable stock. Simmer until tender, then purée.

A hearty and colourful vegetarian meal with subtle spice. The salty Feta perfectly complements the spices and sweet, soft vegetables.

Gently cooked for half an hour, this rich tomato sauce is full of flavour and perfect tossed with gnocchi for an easy weekend supper.

Tomato & Rosemary Gnocchi

Time 45 minutes. Per portion: 447 Kcal, 4g fat (0.8g saturated)

Serves 4

Olive or sunflower oil 1 tbsp

Onion 1, peeled and chopped

Garlic 2 cloves, peeled and finely chopped

Tomatoes 680g (1½lb), skinned (optional) and diced

Rosemary 2–3 stems, plus a little extra to garnish

Tomato purée 1 tbsp

Caster sugar 2 tsp

Cheap red wine and **vegetable stock** mixed half and half 150ml (¼ pint) total or all vegetable stock if preferred

Salt and freshly ground black pepper

Chilled gnocchi 2 x 500g (1lb 2oz) packs

Cheddar cheese grated, to serve

Scan the **QR Code** with a smartphone for an ingredients shopping list

Heat the oil in a saucepan over a medium heat and fry the onion for about 5 minutes until softened. Stir in the garlic, tomatoes and rosemary and cook for a few minutes, then mix in the tomato purée, sugar and the wine and stock mix. Season well with salt and pepper.

Reduce the heat, cover and simmer for 30 minutes, stirring occasionally, until the tomatoes are pulpy and the sauce has thickened.

When the sauce is almost ready, bring a large saucepan of lightly salted water to the boil. Add the gnocchi and cook for 2–3 minutes or according to the packet's directions until they float to the surface of the water and are hot.

Drain the gnocchi well in a colander then return them to the pan, add the tomato sauce and stir together gently. Spoon into warmed shallow bowls, sprinkle with a little extra snipped fresh rosemary, if using, and sprinkle with the grated cheese.

Cook's tips

Gnocchi can be bought in the supermarket chilled or dried and is usually found in the pasta aisle. It can be made at home by mixing mashed potato with flour, baking powder and egg, then shaping into ropes and snipping into bite-sized pieces. Chill before poaching.

Creamy Vegetable Crumble

(V) (F)

Time 1 hour. Per portion: 569 Kcal, 27g fat (15.5g saturated)

Serves 4

Vegetable stock cubes 2

Sweet potatoes 2, peeled and cut into chunks

Carrots 2, peeled and cut into chunks

Parsnips 2, peeled and cut into chunks

Leeks 2, washed and cut into thick slices

Sweetcorn 198g can, drained

Cornflour 1 tbsp (optional)

Soft goat's cheese 110g packet

Salt and freshly ground black pepper

Plain flour 110g (4oz)

Butter 50g (2oz), cubed

Mature Cheddar cheese 110g (4oz), grated

Scan the **QR Code** with a smartphone for an ingredients shopping list

Preheat the oven to 220°C/425°F/Gas 7. Pour 1 litre (1¾ pints) of water into a large saucepan and bring it to the boil. Crumble in the stock cubes and stir until they have dissolved.

Add the potatoes and carrots. Bring the mixture to the boil, then cover, reduce the heat and allow to simmer for 5 minutes. Add the parsnips and leeks.

Re-cover the pan and bring back to the boil, then reduce the heat and simmer for 10–15 minutes until tender. Using a slotted spoon, transfer the vegetables to an ovenproof dish, reserving the cooking liquor. Scatter the sweetcorn over the top of the vegetables.

Bring the cooking liquid to a rapid boil, uncovered, and boil to reduce the quantity by about half. If necessary, thicken with cornflour. Remove the pan from the heat and crumble in the goat's cheese. Stir until the cheese melts, to form a sauce. Season to taste and pour over the vegetables in the dish.

To make the topping, sift the flour into a bowl, add the butter and rub it in with your fingertips until the mixture resembles coarse breadcrumbs, then stir in the Cheddar cheese. Sprinkle this crumble mixture over the vegetables and bake for 20–25 minutes until the topping is golden and the sauce is bubbling. Serve the dish immediately.

Cook's tip

Try using different cheeses as variations. Choose which is on offer – a soft cheese with garlic and herbs is good in the sauce, and Stilton works well in the topping in place of the Cheddar.

Crumbles are not just for pudding. This is an extremely delicious way of getting several of your five-a-day in one meal.

A light buttery tart, which is
perfect for using up any leftover
cheeses and chutney.

Two Cheese and Onion Tart

(V) (F)

Time 40 minutes. Per portion: 614 Kcal, 41g fat (20.8g saturated)

Serves 3

Ready-rolled puff pastry
320g pack

Tomato chutney or ketchup
3 tbsp

Onion 1, peeled and thinly
sliced

**Cheddar cheese, Double
Gloucester or Red Leicester**
mixed with a blue cheese like
Gorgonzola or Stilton 150g
(5oz), cut into cubes

Baby plum or cherry tomatoes
10, halved

Freshly ground black pepper

Chopped parsley to garnish
(optional)

Green salad to serve (optional)

Scan the **QR Code** with
a smartphone for an
ingredients shopping list

Preheat the oven to 220°C/425°F/Gas 7. Carefully
unroll the pastry and put the sheet (measuring 23 x
35cm/9 x 14in) on to a heavy baking sheet.

With a sharp knife, mark a border about 1.5cm (½in)
in from the edge all round and lightly mark it for
decoration. With a fork, prick inside the border, to keep
the pastry flat while it cooks.

Spread the chutney or ketchup inside the border,
then scatter the onion slices over the sauce, followed
by the cheese cubes and tomato halves. Season with
black pepper.

Bake the tart in the bottom half of the oven for about
30 minutes until the pastry is browned and crispy.
Cool for a few minutes and then sprinkle with a little
parsley, if using. Serve the tart warm or cold with a
crisp green salad, if you like.

Cook's tip

This is easy to assemble and can be left in the fridge, loosely covered
with cling film, ready for baking when you need it.

Rich Lemon Chicken

Time 55 minutes. Per portion: 238 Kcal, 10g fat (2.8g saturated)

Serves 4

Olive or sunflower oil 1 tbsp

Chicken thighs 1kg (2¼lb) or 6, skinned, boned, meat cut into chunks

Onion 1, peeled and chopped

Lemon 1, grated zest and juice

Chicken stock 300ml (½ pint)

Fresh thyme sprigs 2, or ½ tsp dried

Salt and freshly ground black pepper

Egg yolks 2

Parsley or chives small bunch, finely chopped

Cooked macaroni or small pasta shapes to serve (optional)

Scan the **QR Code** with a smartphone for an ingredients shopping list

Heat the oil in a large lidded frying pan over a medium-high heat and add the cubed chicken. Fry for about 5 minutes, stirring occasionally, until lightly browned.

Push the chicken to one side of the pan, then add the onion and fry for 5 minutes until softened.

Add the lemon zest and juice, then the stock, thyme and a little salt and pepper. Bring to the boil, stirring, then reduce the heat, cover and simmer for 30 minutes, stirring occasionally.

Scoop the chicken out of the pan with a slotted spoon and keep warm. Beat the egg yolks together in a bowl, then gradually beat in the hot stock and onions until smooth. Return the sauce to the pan and cook over a low heat, stirring constantly until it has lightly thickened.

Return the chicken to the pan and stir in the chopped herbs. Serve with cooked pasta, if using.

Cook's tips

Be careful not to overheat the sauce at the end when thickening with the egg yolks; if it boils, they will curdle. If you are short of time, you may prefer to use 600g (1lb 5oz) of ready-diced chicken thigh meat, chicken breast mini fillets or turkey breast slices.

A traditional Greek dish, which combines
simple ingredients to create a fresh
and flavourful meal.

A mild, delicately flavoured curry gently simmered
on the hob with yogurt. So tasty, you will never
need to splash out on an Indian take-away again.

Kashmiri Butter Chicken

F

Time 55 minutes. Per portion: 325 Kcal, 16g fat (6.8g saturated)

Serves 4

Sunflower oil 1 tbsp

Chicken thighs 1kg (2¼lb) or 6, skinned, boned, meat cut into chunks

Butter 25g (1oz)

Onion 1, peeled, quartered and finely chopped

Garlic 2 cloves, peeled and finely chopped

Root ginger 2.5cm (1in) piece, peeled and finely chopped

Korma (mild) curry paste 4 tbsp

Plain flour 1 tbsp

Tomato purée 1 tbsp

Plain yogurt 150g (5oz)

Chicken stock 200ml (7fl oz)

Salt and freshly ground black pepper

Pilau rice to serve (optional)

Chopped coriander and flaked almonds to garnish (optional)

 Scan the **QR Code** with a smartphone for an ingredients shopping list

Heat the oil in a large lidded frying pan over a medium-high heat and add the cubed chicken. Fry for about 5 minutes, stirring occasionally, until the chicken is lightly browned.

Push the chicken to one side of the pan, then add the butter, onion, garlic and ginger and cook for about 3 minutes until softened. Stir in the curry paste and cook for a further 2 minutes.

Mix the flour and tomato purée into the yogurt, reduce the heat, then stir into the frying pan. Gradually mix in the stock and season with salt and pepper. Cover and simmer for 30 minutes, stirring occasionally.

Serve the chicken on a bed of rice and garnish, if liked, with coriander and toasted flaked almonds.

Cook's tips

It is much cheaper to buy chicken thighs on the bone. It doesn't take long to remove the skin and cut away the bones – if you don't like the feel of raw meat, wear your washing up gloves. Alternatively, use 600g (1lb 5oz) boneless chicken thigh meat if preferred.

Pesto Chicken
with Petits Potatoes

Time 50 minutes. Per portion: 635 Kcal, 37g fat (10.5g saturated)

Serves 2

Potatoes 400g (14oz), peeled and cubed

Olive oil 4 tbsp

Skinless chicken breasts 2, cut into finger-width strips

Crème fraîche 3 tbsp

Pesto 2 tbsp

Scan the **QR Code** with a smartphone for an ingredients shopping list

Preheat the oven to 200°C/400°F/Gas 6 and heat a shallow roasting tin or tray. Bring a saucepan of lightly salted water to the boil and add the potatoes. Bring back to the boil, cook for 5 minutes and drain well.

Spoon 3 tbsp of the oil into the roasting tin and toss in the potato cubes. Roast for 40 minutes, turning them a few times so that they crisp and brown all over.

Meanwhile, heat a wok or large frying pan over a medium heat, pour in the remaining oil and add the chicken strips in one layer. Cook for 2–3 minutes until the strips are brown then turn over and cook for another couple of minutes.

Add 2 tbsp crème fraîche and the pesto to the frying pan and simmer gently for 5 minutes. Add 1 tablespoon more of crème fraîche then serve the chicken strips with the roast potatoes.

Cook's tip

If you have some leftover herbs, make your own pesto: in a food processor, whizz 50g (2oz) of herbs, such as basil or parsley, with 15g (½oz) of pine nuts or walnuts, 1 clove of garlic, 3 tbsp grated Parmesan and 5 tbsp olive oil.

This is so simple yet looks (and tastes) good enough to cook for friends; just double or triple the quantity.

Cosy comfort food to satisfy the whole family.
This delicious pie is perfect for making use of
any leftover meat from your Sunday roast.

Chicken, Mushroom & Ham Pie

(F)

Time 55 minutes. Per portion: 657 Kcal, 48g fat (23.6g saturated)

Serves 6

Cooked chicken or turkey 225g (8oz), chopped

Ham, thickly sliced 150g (5oz), chopped

Button mushrooms 200g pack, wiped and quartered

Sweetcorn 198g can, drained

Soft cheese with herbs 200g tub

Stock cube 1 ham or chicken

Double cream 150ml pot

Salt and freshly ground black pepper

Puff pastry 375g packet, thawed if frozen

Egg 1, beaten

Mash and cooked carrots and green beans to serve (optional)

Scan the **QR Code** with a smartphone for an ingredients shopping list

Preheat the oven to 220°C/425°F/Gas 7. Place the chicken, ham, mushrooms and sweetcorn in the base of a pie dish (about 1.25 litres/2 pint capacity), and stir them to mix. Spoon over the soft cheese.

Dissolve the stock cube in 4 tbsp boiling water and then stir in the cream and seasoning. Pour this mixture into the pie dish.

Roll out the pastry on a lightly floured surface until it is just larger than the pie dish. Cut around the edges to give a 1.5cm (½in) strip, brush water over the rim of the pie dish and then stick the strip of pastry on it. Brush water over the pastry rim and then lift the large piece over the top. Press it well around the edges.

Trim around the dish with a sharp knife to remove any excess. Use a sharp knife to make lots of cuts around the pastry edge to help the pastry rise. If liked, add decorative pastry leaves. Make a hole in the pastry in the centre of the pie to allow steam to escape. Brush with beaten egg and then bake in the centre of the oven for 30–40 minutes, or until the pastry is golden in colour and the filling is bubbling hot.

Remove the pie from the oven and serve with mash, steamed carrots and green beans, if you like.

Cook's tips

Shop-bought pies can be pretty tasteless, and if you buy from an artisan producer, very expensive. Treat yourself to this homemade version. It's very filling and so you will only need mash as an accompaniment if your guests are very hungry, otherwise just stick with steamed vegetables.

Turkey Gumbo

F

Time 50 minutes. Per portion: 245 Kcal, 6.8g fat (1.2g saturated)

Serves 4

Sunflower oil 1 tbsp

Turkey breast steaks 400g (14oz), cubed

Smoked streaky bacon 3 rashers, diced

Onion 1, peeled and chopped

Celery sticks 2, thickly sliced

Tomatoes 2, diced

Garlic 2 cloves, peeled and finely chopped

Paprika 1 tsp

Dried crushed chillies ¼–½ tsp to taste

Salt

Plain flour 1 tbsp

Chicken stock 450ml (¾ pint)

Bay leaves 2

Thyme sprigs 2–3 or 1 tsp dried

Frozen sweetcorn 200g (7oz)

Okra or green beans 110g (4oz), thickly sliced

Cooked rice to serve (optional)

Heat the oil in a large lidded frying pan over a medium heat and fry the turkey for about 5 minutes until just beginning to brown. Add the bacon and onion and fry until golden.

Stir in the celery, tomatoes, garlic, paprika, dried crushed chillies and salt and cook for a minute or two, then mix in the flour. Gradually mix in the stock, then add the herbs and bring to the boil. Reduce the heat, cover and simmer for 25 minutes, stirring occasionally.

Add the sweetcorn and okra or green beans, re-cover and cook for 5 minutes. Remove the bay leaves and serve in warmed bowls with rice, if using.

 Scan the **QR Code** with a smartphone for an ingredients shopping list

Cook's tips

This gumbo has many variations, so mix and match ingredients to suit what you have or what you prefer. If you have a little spiced chorizo-style sausage, add this in place of the bacon; half a pepper would also be a good addition, or try the recipe with diced chicken thigh meat instead of the turkey.

This New Orleans dish is a thick stew of meat,
vegetables and rice, and is perfect for using
up leftovers you may have in your fridge.

Transform a very cheap turkey drumstick into a hearty supper full of Middle Eastern promise.

Slow-Cooked Turkey with Spiced Chickpeas

Ⓕ

Time 2¾ hours. Per portion: 353 Kcal, 12g fat (2.6g saturated)

Serves 4

Turkey drumstick about 700g (1lb 10oz) in total

Sunflower oil 1 tbsp

Onion 1, peeled and chopped

Garlic 2 cloves, peeled and finely chopped

Root ginger 4cm (1½in) piece, peeled and finely chopped

Ground cumin 1 tsp

Ground turmeric 1 tsp

Ground mixed spice 1 tsp

Dried crushed chillies ½-1 tsp

Chopped tomatoes 400g can

Chickpeas 410g can, drained

Chicken stock 600ml (1 pint)

Raisins or sultanas 50g (2oz)

Freshly ground black pepper

Carrots 350g (12oz), diced

Curly kale 110g (4oz), sliced

Cooked rice or couscous to serve (optional)

Scan the **QR Code** with a smartphone for an ingredients shopping list

Partially sever the knuckle end of the turkey drumstick by using a large knife and hitting it with a rolling pin or hammer so that the knuckle can be bent round and will fit in a large saucepan. Put it in the pan with the oil and fry for about 5 minutes, turning until browned. When the drumstick has begun to colour, add the onion and cook for a further 5 minutes.

Add the garlic, ginger, ground spices and chillies and cook for 1 minute more, then mix in the tomatoes, chickpeas, stock and dried fruit. Season with pepper and bring to the boil, stirring the sauce to mix.

Reduce the heat, cover and simmer for 2 hours or until the turkey is almost falling off the bone. Lift the drumstick out of the pan and put on to a plate. Add the carrots to the pan and cook uncovered for 15 minutes until just tender.

Meanwhile, remove the skin, tendons and bone from the turkey, then cut the meat into pieces return to the pan.

Add the kale and cook for a few minutes until just wilted. Spoon the stew into warmed shallow bowls lined with couscous or rice, if using.

Cook's tips

The ingredients list may look long but the jars keep for ages and root ginger can be chopped and frozen or kept in the salad compartment of the fridge for several weeks. If you have runner beans, slice and add some in place of the kale and cook for about 10 minutes until just tender.

Roast Duck with Apples & Potatoes

Ⓕ

Time 1½ hours. Per portion: 735 Kcal, 43g fat (11.8g saturated)

Serves 4

Potatoes 4, about 680g (1½lb), scrubbed and thinly sliced

Onions 2, peeled and thinly sliced

Sharp dessert apples 2, such as Braeburn or Granny Smith, cored and thickly sliced

Thyme 3 sprigs or 1 tsp dried

Salt and freshly ground black pepper

Duck legs 4

Chicken stock 300ml (½ pint)

Steamed green vegetables to serve (optional)

Scan the **QR Code** with a smartphone for an ingredients shopping list

Preheat the oven to 180°C/350°F/Gas 4. Arrange the potatoes, onions and apples in the base of a roasting tin. Sprinkle the leaves from half the thyme over the tin and season generously with salt and pepper.

Arrange the duck joints on top, then season these with salt, pepper and the remaining thyme. Pour the stock into the base of the tin, then roast in the oven for 1–1¼ hours until the duck and potatoes are golden and tender. The juices should run clear when the duck is pierced through the thickest part with a sharp knife.

Transfer the duck joints to a plate, cover with foil and keep hot. Brown the top of the potatoes under the grill, if needed, then spoon on to warmed plates with some of the pan juices, top with the duck joints and serve with steamed green vegetables, if liked.

Cook's tip

If you really want to push the boat out, use duck breasts instead of duck legs.
It will increase the cost of the dish by around 50 per cent.

Impress friends when they come to dinner without spending a fortune. Duck leg joints are very reasonable and can taste just as delicious as duck breasts.

This quiche makes perfect picnic or packed lunch fare – much more exciting than a plain old cheese or ham sandwich.

Pea & Ham Quiche

(F)

Time 1 hour. Per portion: 608 Kcal, 44g fat (22.1g saturated)

Serves 6

Ready-made shortcrust pastry 375g (13oz)

Eggs 4, beaten

Crème fraîche 250ml tub

Salt and freshly ground black pepper

Frozen peas 110g (4oz), defrosted

Spring onions 3, trimmed and finely chopped

Ham 250g (9oz), chopped into chunks

Double Gloucester cheese 75g (3oz), grated

Mixed leaf salad to serve (optional)

Scan the **QR Code** with a smartphone for an ingredients shopping list

Preheat the oven to 200°C/400°F/Gas 6.

Fold the pastry in half and then roll out until a little larger than a 23cm (9in) fluted flan tin. Lift the pastry over the rolling pin, drape in the tin then ease up the sides pressing it in place with your fingertips. Trim the top of the pastry so that it stands a little above the top of the tin. Prick the base of the pastry and then chill for 15 minutes.

Line the pastry case with non-stick baking paper and baking beans and bake blind for 15 minutes.

Meanwhile, in a jug, mix together the eggs and crème fraîche and season well with salt and pepper.

Remove the paper and beans from the pastry case and reduce the oven temperature to 180°C/350°F/Gas 4. Pour in the creamy mixture and then evenly sprinkle in the peas, spring onions, ham and grated cheese.

Return the quiche to the oven and bake for 25–30 minutes, until it is just set and golden. Serve with a mixed salad if you like.

Cook's tips

If time is short, choose ready-rolled shortcrust pastry, although it does cost a little more to buy. The leftover eggs, peas and spring onions in this dish can be used to make a delicious egg fried rice: simply pan fry with cooked rice and add a dash of soy sauce.

Pork Bolognese

F

Time 50 minutes. Per portion: 193 Kcal, 5g fat (1.7g saturated)

Serves 6

Lean minced pork 500g (1lb 2oz)

Onion 1, peeled and finely chopped

Carrot 1, peeled and finely diced

Red pepper 1, deseeded and diced

Garlic 1–2 cloves, peeled and finely chopped

Mushrooms 110g (4oz), wiped and chopped

Dried oregano or mixed herbs 1 rounded tsp

Chopped tomatoes 400g can

Vegetable or chicken stock 225ml (8fl oz)

Tomato ketchup 1 tbsp

Bay leaves 2

Green beans 110g (4oz), chopped into small pieces

Spaghetti 75g (3oz) per person

Chicken gravy granules 2 tsp

Grated Parmesan cheese to serve (optional)

 Scan the **QR Code** with a smartphone for an ingredients shopping list

Heat a deep frying pan. Add the pork mince and cook over a medium heat for 5 minutes until browned all over.

Add the onion, carrot, red pepper and garlic and cook for 5 minutes, covered, before adding the mushrooms and herbs. Cook for another 5 minutes and then pour in the tomatoes and stock and stir in the ketchup, bay leaves and beans. Simmer, uncovered, for 20 minutes.

Bring a large saucepan of water to the boil and cook the spaghetti according to the packet's instructions.

A few minutes before serving, sprinkle the gravy granules into the mince to thicken the sauce. Remove the bay leaves.

Drain the spaghetti, divide between hot bowls and spoon the sauce on top. Serve with a little freshly grated Parmesan if you like.

Cook's tip

This is perfect for freezing. Store, in portions, in plastic containers then simply move from freezer to fridge the night before your meal. Heat until piping hot in a saucepan or the microwave.

This is a delicious and healthy alternative to standard Bolognese. The recipe makes a big batch, so you can freeze some and enjoy several meals with little effort.

This is a great weekend supper; you can pop it in the oven and take the dog out for a walk or the kids to the park and if you get a little delayed, the meal won't spoil.

Pork & Cranberry Hotpot

Time 2½ hours. Per portion: 558 Kcal, 25g fat (9.9g saturated)

Serves 4

Sunflower oil 1 tbsp

Pork shoulder steaks or boneless pork spare rib chops 4, about 700g (1lb 10oz) in total

Onion 1, peeled and chopped

Plain flour 2 tbsp

Chicken stock 450ml (¾ pint)

Sherry 4 tbsp (optional)

Tomato purée 1 tbsp

Cranberry sauce 2 tbsp

Dried cranberries 25g (1oz) (optional)

Ground allspice ½ tsp

Salt and freshly ground black pepper

Potatoes 600g (1lb 5oz), peeled and thinly sliced

Butter 25g (1oz)

Steamed peas or green beans to serve (optional)

Scan the **QR Code** with a smartphone for an ingredients shopping list

Preheat the oven to 180°C/350°F/Gas 4. Heat the oil in a large frying pan over a medium heat and fry the pork for about 2 minutes on each side until browned. Lift the meat out of the pan with a slotted spoon and transfer to a shallow flameproof casserole dish.

Add the onion to the pan and fry for about 5 minutes until softened and just beginning to turn golden. Stir in the flour then mix in the stock, sherry, if using, tomato purée and cranberry sauce. Mix in the cranberries, if using, then add the spice and a generous sprinkle of salt and pepper.

Bring the sauce to the boil, then pour it over the pork. Arrange the potato slices overlapping over the top, sprinkle with a little extra salt and pepper then dot with the butter.

Cover with a lid or foil and bake for 1½ hours. Remove the lid or foil and cook for 30 minutes more until the potatoes are golden. Spoon into shallow bowls and serve with steamed peas or green beans, if using.

Cook's tips

If you are going out, take the lid off when you get home and brown the potatoes under the grill for a few minutes instead. Add leftover cranberries to oats with some grated apple and raisins for a delicious breakfast cereal.

Pork, Chorizo & Bean Casserole

F

Time 2 hours. Per portion: 765 Kcal, 47g fat (17.9g saturated)

Serves 4

Pork belly slices 680g (1½lb), cubed

Chorizo sausage 110g (4oz), diced

Onion 1, peeled and chopped

Garlic 2 cloves, peeled and finely chopped

Plain flour 1 tbsp

Chopped tomatoes 400g can

Cannellini or haricot beans 410g can, drained

Chicken stock 450ml (¾ pint)

Potatoes 450g (1lb), scrubbed and cut into 2.5 cm (1in) chunks

Rosemary 2 sprigs

Salt and freshly ground black pepper

Runner beans 3, thinly sliced

Chopped parsley or chives to serve (optional)

 Scan the **QR Code** with a smartphone for an ingredients shopping list

Preheat the oven to 180°C/350°F/Gas 4. Heat a large frying pan over a low heat, and fry the belly pork and chorizo for about 5 minutes until the fat begins to run. Add the onion, increase the heat to medium and fry for 5 more minutes, stirring until the onion is just turning golden.

Add the garlic and cook for 1 minute, then stir in the flour. Add the tomatoes, beans and stock and mix together, then add the potatoes and rosemary. Season with salt and pepper and bring to the boil.

Transfer the mixture to an ovenproof casserole dish, cover and bake in the oven for about 1¼ hours until the pork is very tender.

Stir the stew then arrange the runner beans on top, re-cover and cook for 15 minutes. Remove the rosemary sprigs and spoon into warmed bowls and garnish with the parsley or chives, if you like.

Cook's tip

For a speedier version of this dish, add a 350g (12oz) pack of chilled frankfurters instead of the belly pork and cook on the hob for 30 minutes.

Pork belly slices, sometimes called pork streaky rashers, are great value and when mixed with chorizo, beans and potato make a hearty stew with generously sized portions.

Succulent ribs served in a sweet and spicy
sticky sauce – simply irresistible.

Sticky Ribs with Baked Potatoes

Time 1½ hours. Per portion: 433 Kcal, 21g fat (5.9g saturated)

Serves 2

Pork ribs pack of 6

Sunflower oil 1 tbsp

Tomato ketchup 2 tbsp

Paprika 1 tsp

Ground cumin ½ tsp

Chilli powder ¼ tsp

Salt and freshly ground black pepper

Baking potatoes 2, scrubbed and pricked

Cooked corn on the cob 2, to serve (optional)

Scan the **QR Code** with a smartphone for an ingredients shopping list

Preheat the oven to 200°C/400°F/Gas 6 and line a small roasting tin with foil.

Place the ribs in the roasting tin and add a splash of water to the base of the tin. Mix the oil, ketchup, paprika, cumin and chilli with salt and pepper and spoon over the ribs.

Place the ribs on the shelf just above the centre of the oven for 1¼-1½ hours. Bake the potatoes alongside the ribs. Turn the ribs halfway through cooking and brush with the pan juice mixture.

Serve the cooked ribs and potatoes with corn on the cob if you like.

Cook's tip

Ribs are often included in multibuy offers at the supermarket. Buy a couple of packs and freeze one. Try coleslaw as an accompaniment instead of corn on the cob.

Sausage & Baked Bean Stew

(F)

Time 1¾ hours. Per portion: 560 Kcal, 33g fat (15.2g saturated)

Serves 4

Butter 50g (2oz)

Lincolnshire sausages 450g (1lb)

Onion 1, peeled and sliced

Smoked streaky bacon 6 rashers, chopped

Chopped tomatoes 400g can

Baked beans 425g can

Pork or ham stock cube 1, crumbled

Fresh white breadcrumbs 50g (2oz)

Garlic 1 clove, peeled and crushed

Chopped parsley 1 tbsp or 1 tsp dried mixed herbs

Green salad to serve (optional)

Scan the **QR Code** with a smartphone for an ingredients shopping list

Preheat the oven to 180°C/350°F/Gas 4. Melt the butter in a frying pan over a medium heat, pour half of it into a small bowl and then fry the sausages for 6–8 minutes until they have browned. Remove the sausages from the pan and place in a casserole dish.

Add the onion and bacon to the pan and cook for about 5 minutes until the onion starts to soften.

Stir in the chopped tomatoes, baked beans and stock cube. Pour the mixture into the casserole dish and mix together.

To make the topping, tip the breadcrumbs into a bowl and stir in the remaining melted butter, garlic and parsley or mixed herbs. Sprinkle the topping over the sausages and then bake in the centre of the oven for 50 minutes–1 hour, until the topping is golden in colour. Serve the stew with a fresh green salad, if using.

Cook's tip

To avoid having to throw fresh herbs away, cultivate them yourself. Keep a few pots of your favourites on the kitchen windowsill in winter and by the back door in summer.

This hearty dish is a winner with all the family. Pop it in the oven and spend some quality time together while it cooks.

Vibrant red vegetables slow-cooked to a
wonderful tenderness and served with
roasted sausages – perfect comfort food.

Braised Red Cabbage with Sausages

F

Time 2½ hours. Per portion: 210 Kcal, 11g fat (3.8g saturated)

Serves 6

Sunflower oil 1 tbsp

Onion 1, peeled and chopped

Red cabbage 300g (11oz), thinly sliced

Raw beetroot 300g (11oz), trimmed, peeled and diced

Orange 1, grated zest and juice

Caster sugar 2 tbsp

Red or white wine vinegar 2 tbsp

Hot vegetable stock 300ml (½ pint)

Ground allspice 1 tsp

Salt and freshly ground black pepper

Pork & Apple Sausages 12

Scan the **QR Code** with a smartphone for an ingredients shopping list

Preheat the oven to 180°C/350°F/Gas 4. Heat the oil in a frying pan over a medium heat and fry the onion for about 5 minutes until softened.

Transfer the onion to a casserole dish, add the cabbage and beetroot and then mix in all the remaining ingredients (except the sausages).

Cover, place on a baking tray and cook in the oven for 2–2¼ hours until tender.

Meanwhile, place a wire rack on a baking tray and space out the sausages on the rack evenly. Place the baking tray in the oven above the cabbage for the last 30 minutes of cooking time, turning halfway through. Check the sausages are cooked, then serve.

Cook's tips

A mix of red cabbage and beetroot has been used here, but double quantity of just one of the vegetables could be cooked this way if preferred. Wear rubber gloves when preparing the beetroot. Pork and chilli sausages also work really well in this dish.

Greek-Style Lamb

F

Time 3 hours. Per portion: 524 Kcal, 20g fat (8g saturated)

Serves 4

Olive or sunflower oil 1 tbsp

Lamb neck fillet or stewing lamb on the bone 750g (1lb 10oz)

Onions 2, peeled and chopped

Garlic 2 cloves, peeled and finely chopped

Coriander seeds 2 tsp, crushed

Plain flour 2 tbsp

Lamb stock 600ml (1 pint)

Honey 1 tbsp

Lemon 1, thinly sliced

Bay leaves 2

Salt and freshly ground black pepper

Potatoes 680g (1½lb), peeled and thickly sliced

Mixed frozen broad beans and peas 225g (8oz)

Chopped parsley to garnish (optional)

Scan the **QR Code** with a smartphone for an ingredients shopping list

Preheat the oven to 180°C/350°F/Gas 4. Heat the oil in a large frying pan over a medium heat and fry the lamb for about 5 minutes until evenly browned, turning as needed. Transfer the meat to a plate.

Add the onion to the pan and fry for about 5 minutes until lightly browned. Stir in the garlic and coriander seeds, then mix in the flour.

Gradually pour in the stock and bring to the boil, stirring. Add the honey, lemon slices and bay leaves and season generously with salt and pepper.

Arrange the potatoes in the base of a casserole dish, then place the lamb on top and pour over the hot stock. Cover with a lid or foil and bake in the oven for about 2½ hours until the lamb is very tender.

Just before serving, add the frozen vegetables to a saucepan of boiling water, cook for 4–5 minutes then drain and toss with the parsley, if using. To serve, remove the bay leaves, spoon the lamb, potatoes and sauce into warmed serving bowls and place the vegetables on top.

Cook's tip

This recipe is made with cut-price lamb neck, but if the budget allows it, you may like to splash out and use four small lamb shanks instead.

Flavoured with crushed coriander seeds, bay leaves and sliced lemons, then cooked long and slow, this Greek-inspired dish gives meltingly tender lamb.

Stretch a good cut of lamb with canned
chickpeas and rice for a filling supper
suffused with Moroccan spices.

Spiced Lamb Pilaf

Time 1 hour. Per portion: 535 Kcal, 20g fat (7.4g saturated)

Serves 4

Olive or sunflower oil 1 tbsp

Onion 1, peeled and chopped

Lamb chump chops or lamb fillet 300g (11oz), dlced

Garlic 2 cloves, peeled and finely chopped (optional)

Ground cinnamon 1 tsp

Paprika 1 tsp

Cumin seeds 1 tsp, crushed

Easy cook brown rice 225g (8oz)

Chickpeas 410g can, drained

Raisins 65g (2½oz)

Lamb stock 1.2 litres (2 pints)

Salt and freshly ground black pepper

Greek-style plain yogurt to serve (optional)

Fried onions to serve (optional)

Torn mint leaves to serve (optional)

Heat the oil in a large frying pan over a medium heat and fry the onion and lamb for about 5 minutes until the lamb is browned all over and the onion golden.

Stir in the garlic, if using, the spices and then the rice and cook for 1 minute. Mix in the chickpeas, raisins, half the stock and a generous amount of salt and pepper. Cover and cook gently for 40–45 minutes, stirring from time to time and topping up with the remaining stock as needed until the rice is tender.

Spoon the pilaf into warmed serving bowls, top with spoonfuls of yogurt, the fried onions and a few torn mint leaves, if using.

Scan the **QR Code** with a smartphone for an ingredients shopping list

Cook's tip

Mint is one of the most prolific herbs to grow in the garden or in a tub by the back door. If you don't have any, you could garnish this dish with some toasted flaked almonds instead.

Pesto Meatballs with Spaghetti

Ⓕ

Time 50 minutes. Per portion: 685 Kcal, 27g fat (10.3g saturated)

Serves 4

Bread 1 slice, torn into pieces

Minced beef 500g (1lb 2oz)

Egg yolk 1

Salt and freshly ground black pepper

Olive or sunflower oil 1 tbsp

Onion 1, peeled and chopped

Garlic 2 cloves, peeled and finely chopped

Chopped tomatoes 400g can

Beef stock 150ml (¼ pint)

Pesto sauce 1 tbsp

Caster sugar 1 tsp

Dried spaghetti 350g (12oz)

Basil leaves to garnish (optional)

Scan the **QR Code** with a smartphone for an ingredients shopping list

Make the bread into crumbs in a food processor, then add the mince, egg yolk and plenty of salt and pepper. Mix together then tip the mixture out onto a chopping board, divide it into 20 spoonfuls and roll into balls with wet hands.

Heat the oil in a large frying pan over a medium heat and cook the meatballs for 5–8 minutes until browned on all sides. Lift them out of the pan with a slotted spoon and put onto a plate.

Add the onion to the frying pan and cook for 5 minutes until softened and lightly browned. Add the garlic, tomatoes, stock, pesto, sugar and a little salt and pepper and bring to the boil, stirring.

Return the meatballs to the frying pan, reduce the heat, cover and simmer for 20 minutes, turning the meatballs once or twice until cooked.

Meanwhile, bring a large saucepan of water to the boil, add the spaghetti and cook according to the packet's instructions. Drain and return to the dry pan. Add the meatballs and sauce, then spoon into bowls and sprinkle with basil leaves, if using.

Cook's tip

If you don't have a food processor or liquidiser make the breadcrumbs by grating the bread, then mix with the mince, egg yolk and seasoning in a bowl.

A refreshing alternative to Bolognese, these meatballs are the perfect storecupboard standby – just pop a pack of mince in your shopping basket.

Cottage pie is one of those timeless favourites; this version is flavoured with a little curry powder and mixed with red lentils to produce a delicious take on a classic.

Spiced Cottage Pie

F

Time 50 minutes. Per portion: 737 Kcal, 25g fat (10.8g saturated)

Serves 6

Sunflower oil 1 tbsp

Minced beef 500g (1lb 2oz)

Onion 1, peeled and chopped

Medium hot curry powder 2 tbsp

Carrot 150g (5oz), diced

Red lentils 150g (5oz)

Beef stock 600ml (1 pint)

Tomato purée 1 tbsp

Sultanas 50g (2oz)

Salt and freshly ground black pepper

Potatoes 680g (1½lb), peeled and cut into chunks

Butter 50g (2oz)

Milk 4 tbsp

Ground turmeric ¼ tsp

Cooked frozen peas to serve (optional)

Scan the **QR Code** with a smartphone for an ingredients shopping list

Heat the oil in a saucepan over a medium heat and fry the mince and onion, stirring and breaking up the mince, for about 5 minutes until it is evenly browned.

Stir in the curry powder and carrot, cook 1 minute and then mix in the lentils. Pour in the stock, tomato purée, sultanas and seasoning and bring to the boil.

Cover and simmer for 25 minutes, stirring occasionally until the lentils are soft.

Meanwhile, put the potatoes into a saucepan with just enough lightly salted water to cover them. Cover with the lid and bring the water to the boil. Then reduce the heat and simmer for about 15 minutes until the potatoes are tender.

Drain the potatoes, return them to the pan with half the butter and the milk and turmeric and season with salt and pepper. Mash well, adding the milk as needed to make a soft spoonable mash.

Preheat the grill to hot. Spoon the mince mixture into an ovenproof dish, cover with the potato and fork the mash into an even layer. Dot the remaining butter over the top and grill for 5–10 minutes until browned. Serve with peas, if you like.

Cook's tip

Leftover lentils can be used to make a delicious, filling soup. Cook 110g (4oz) lentils with 1 chopped potato, carrot, onion and parsnip (or any other leftover veg you fancy) and 900ml (1½ pints) stock very gently for 1 hour. Purée with a stick blender before you serve.

Slow-Cooked Asian Beef

F

Time 2½ hours. Per portion: 527 Kcal, 19g fat (4.4g saturated)

Serves 4

Sunflower oil 2 tbsp

Diced stewing beef 500g (1lb 2oz)

Onion 1, peeled and sliced

Plain flour 2 tbsp

Beef stock 600ml (1 pint)

Soy sauce 4 tbsp

White wine vinegar 4 tbsp

Caster sugar 2 tbsp

Bay leaves 2

Black peppercorns 1 tsp, roughly crushed

Salt

Dried egg noodles 200g (7oz)

Ready prepared stir-fry vegetable mix 300g (11oz)

Coriander small bunch, torn (optional)

Scan the **QR Code** with a smartphone for an ingredients shopping list

Preheat the oven to 180°C/350°F/Gas 4. Heat 1 tbsp oil in a large frying pan over a medium heat, then fry the beef for a few minutes. Add the onion slices and fry for another 5 minutes, stirring until the meat is browned on all sides and the onion softened.

Stir in the flour, then mix in the stock, soy sauce and vinegar. Add the sugar, bay leaves, crushed peppercorns and a little salt and bring to the boil.

Transfer the mixture to a casserole dish, cover and cook in the oven for 2 hours or until the meat is tender.

When almost ready to serve, add the noodles to a pan of boiling water and cook according to the packet's instructions. Heat the remaining oil in a frying pan or wok, add the stir-fry vegetables and cook for 2–3 minutes, stirring until hot, then mix the coriander (if using) into the vegetables. Spoon the noodles into bowls, top with the beef (remove the bay leaves) then spoon the vegetables on top.

Cook's tips

Packs of ready prepared stir-fry vegetables can work out cheaper than buying the same ingredients separately, especially if you choose a pack from the supermarket's budget or basics range.

Popular in the Philippines, this slow-cooked beef stew is flavoured with soy sauce and served on a bed of egg noodles and topped with tender stir-fried vegetables.

A comforting, filling winter supper that
needs only a very simple accompaniment
of a few frozen beans or peas.

Braised Beef with Stilton Scones

Ⓕ

Time 3 hours. Per portion: 594 Kcal, 29g fat (13.8g saturated)

Serves 4

Sunflower oil 1 tbsp

Diced stewing beef 500g (1lb 2oz)

Onion 1, peeled and chopped

Plain flour 2 tbsp

Beef stock 750ml (1¼ pints)

Tomato purée 1 tbsp

Worcestershire sauce 2 tbsp

Hot horseradish sauce 1 tbsp

Salt and freshly ground black pepper

Self-raising flour 175g (6oz)

Butter 25g (1oz)

Stilton or other strong blue cheese 110g (4oz), crumbled

Egg 1, beaten

Milk 3–4 tbsp

Closed cup mushrooms 110g (4oz), wiped and sliced

Cooked frozen peas to serve (optional)

 Scan the **QR Code** with a smartphone for an ingredients shopping list

Preheat the oven to 180°C/350°F/Gas 4. Heat the oil in a large frying pan and fry the beef for a few minutes. Add the onion and fry for 5 minutes, stirring, until the meat is browned and the onion softened.

Stir in the flour, then mix in the stock, tomato purée, Worcestershire sauce, horseradish sauce and salt and pepper. Bring to the boil, stirring.

Transfer to a casserole dish large enough to hold the stew and scone topping. Cover the dish and cook in the oven for 2 hours or until the meat is tender.

Meanwhile, make the topping. Put the flour, a little salt and pepper and butter into a mixing bowl and rub in the fat until you have fine crumbs. Stir in the cheese, then add nearly all the egg, keeping just enough back to glaze the top. Gradually stir in enough milk to mix to a soft, but not sticky, dough. Knead very lightly then roll out on a lightly floured surface until a little smaller than the top of the casserole dish.

Remove the lid, stir in the mushrooms then cut the scone topping into eight pieces. Arrange on the meat in a single layer and brush with the remaining egg.

Cook, uncovered, for 20–25 minutes until the topping is well risen and golden. Spoon onto warmed plates and serve with peas, if using.

Cook's tip

For a richer sauce, you might like to add some red wine or beer in place of some of the stock.

Oxtail Chilli

(F)

Time 4 hours. Per portion: 410 Kcal, 17g fat (6.3g saturated)

Serves 4

Sunflower oil 1 tbsp

Oxtail 1kg (2¼lb)

Onions 2, peeled and chopped

Garlic 2 cloves, peeled and finely chopped

Dried crushed chillies 1 tsp

Ground cinnamon 1 tsp

Ground cumin 1 tsp

Plain flour 2 tbsp

Beef stock 300ml (½ pint)

Chopped tomatoes 400g can

Red kidney beans 410g can, drained

Granulated sugar 1 tbsp

Red or white wine vinegar 2 tbsp

Bay leaves 2

Salt and freshly ground black pepper

Rice and salsa (see tip) to serve (optional)

Scan the **QR Code** with a smartphone for an ingredients shopping list

Preheat the oven to 160°C/325°F/Gas 3. Heat the oil in a large frying pan over a medium heat and fry the oxtail for about 5 minutes in batches until browned all over. Lift out of the pan with a slotted spoon and transfer to a large casserole dish.

Add the onions to the pan and fry for about 5 minutes until lightly browned, then mix in the garlic.

Stir in the chillies, spices and flour, then gradually mix in the stock. Add the tomatoes, kidney beans, sugar, vinegar and bay leaves and season generously with salt and pepper. Bring to the boil, stirring, then pour the sauce over the oxtail.

Cover and cook in the oven for 3½-4 hours until the oxtail is very tender. Lift the oxtail out of the sauce and remove the meat from the bones using a knife and fork. Return the meat to the casserole, stir to mix, then spoon onto warmed plates lined with rice, removing the bay leaves. Serve with sweetcorn and tomato salsa, if liked (see tip, below).

Cook's tips

For a quick salsa, cook 150g (5oz) frozen sweetcorn in boiling water for 5 minutes. Drain and mix with ½ chopped red onion or 4 sliced spring onions, 1 diced tomato and a small bunch of chopped coriander. If oxtail doesn't appeal then replace it with 680g (1½lb) stewing beef and cook for 2 hours.

This is a good introduction to those new to oxtail.
The meat is so tender at the end of cooking that it is
practically falling off the bone.

Desserts & Bakes

Quick & Easy

Desserts & Bakes

Take it Easy

A super-quick way to whip up a homemade
frozen dessert in five minutes.
Delicious, nutritious and incredibly easy.

Speedy Summer Berry Sorbet

(V)

Time 5 minutes   Per portion: 61 Kcal, 0.2g fat (0g saturated)

Serves 4-6

Assorted frozen small summer berries such as raspberries, blueberries, blackcurrants, redcurrants 500g (1lb 2oz)

Blackcurrant cordial 6 tbsp, undiluted

Mint leaves to decorate (optional)

Scan the **QR Code** with a smartphone for an ingredients shopping list

Just before you are ready to serve this dessert, place the frozen fruits in a food processor or blender along with the blackcurrant cordial. Blend for a few seconds until well crushed and slightly slushy. You may have to blend the fruits a few times in order to crush them up.

Pile the fruit into serving glasses and decorate with mint, if using. Serve immediately.

Cook's tip

Look in the freezer cabinet for frozen fruits – they are usually excellent value for money. Choose small fruits like the berries and currants, and if you want to use larger soft fruits, cut them into smaller pieces so that they will crush in a blender more easily.

Sautéed Bananas

(V)

Time 10 minutes. Per portion: 291 Kcal, 11g fat (6.7g saturated)

Serves 2

Butter 25g (1oz)

Bananas 2, peeled and sliced

Demerara sugar or soft light brown sugar 2 tbsp

Orange ½, grated zest only

Sultanas 25g (1oz)

Vanilla ice cream 2 scoops to serve (optional)

Melt the butter in a frying pan over a medium heat, then add the bananas, sugar, orange zest and sultanas and fry, stirring, for about 4 minutes until the bananas are hot.

Spoon into warmed bowls and serve with the ice cream, if liked.

Scan the **QR Code** with a smartphone for an ingredients shopping list

Cook's tip

Save the leftover orange for tomorrow's breakfast: segment and serve with a few raisins and topped with natural yogurt – healthy and refreshing.

A real winner with the whole family,
this speedy pud makes use of those old
bananas that would otherwise be wasted.

An easy midweek dessert, these pots of fruit coated in yogurt
and topped with a layer of caramelised sugar make
a delicious alternative to the ubiquitous pot of yogurt.

Cheat's Yogurt Brulée

Ⓥ

Time 25 minutes. Per portion: 167 Kcal, 8g fat (5g saturated)

Serves 6

Vegetable oil for brushing

Demerara sugar 50g (2oz)

Kiwi fruit 2, peeled and thinly sliced

Pears 2, peeled, quartered, and thinly sliced

Greek-style plain yogurt 500g tub

Scan the **QR Code** with a smartphone for an ingredients shopping list

Preheat the grill to hot. Line a baking sheet with foil, then place a ramekin dish upside down on top and draw round it. Repeat to make 6 circles in total. Brush the foil lightly with oil and sprinkle inside each circle evenly with demerara sugar.

Put the sugar circles at least 3 inches below the grill for 30 seconds to 1 minute until the sugar has melted and caramelised. Watch carefully, ensuring that the sugar dissolves but does not burn. Set aside to cool for a few minutes and then loosen with a palette knife.

Meanwhile, divide the fruit between six ramekin dishes. Then spoon the yogurt over the fruit and level the surface. Chill until required.

Place the caramel discs on top of the yogurt and serve.

Cook's tip
Vary the fruits depending on what is a good buy, such as a few strawberries or raspberries in season. You could also include some dried fruit and nuts.

Gooseberry & Hazelnut Fool

Ⓥ

Time 30 minutes. Per portion: 241 Kcal, 9g fat (3.4g saturated)

Serves 4

Gooseberries 450g (1lb)

Caster sugar 65g (2½oz)

Custard powder 1 tbsp

Milk 300ml (½ pint)

Hazelnut yogurt 150g (5oz)

Hazelnuts 2 tbsp, chopped

Shortbread biscuits to serve (optional)

Scan the **QR Code** with
a smartphone for an
ingredients shopping list

Cook the gooseberries with 50g (2oz) of the sugar and 2 tablespoons of water in a saucepan over a low heat for 20 minutes until soft. Purée the gooseberries in a liquidiser or food processor.

Meanwhile, blend the custard powder with the remaining sugar and 2 tablespoons of the milk. Bring the remaining milk up to the boil and pour it onto the blended custard powder. Return the mixture to the pan and heat, stirring, until the custard boils and thickens. Allow to cool completely.

Mix the custard, gooseberry purée and yogurt together, then spoon into serving bowls and sprinkle with hazelnuts. Serve with shortbread, if using.

Cook's tips

Substitute the gooseberries for rhubarb if it's available.
You can also try different flavoured yogurts.

If you grow your own gooseberries, this delicious dessert can cost next to nothing to create yet the taste is fit for a king!

The velvety texture of the soft warm fruit contrasts wonderfully with the crunchy biscuit topping in this speedy sweet.

Crunchy Grilled Peaches with Blueberries

(V)

Time 20 minutes. Per portion: 189 Kcal, 6g fat (2.9g saturated)

Serves 4

Peaches or nectarines 4 ripe, halved and stoned

Butter 15g (½oz), softened

Egg yolk 1

Golden caster sugar 40g (1½oz)

Nice biscuits 50g (2oz), crushed

Blueberries 110g (4oz)

Greek-style plain yogurt to serve (optional)

Scan the **QR Code** with a smartphone for an ingredients shopping list

Preheat the grill to hot. Put the peach or nectarine halves onto a baking sheet, cut-side uppermost and grill for about 4 minutes until softened.

Meanwhile, mix together the butter, egg yolk, half the sugar and crushed biscuits. Spoon the mixture into the cavities of the peaches or nectarines, then grill for a further 30–40 seconds, until lightly browned.

Gently heat the blueberries with the remaining sugar and 4 tablespoons of water. Cook gently for about 3 minutes until softened.

Spoon the blueberries into four bowls, then top with the peaches or nectarines. Serve with the Greek-style yogurt, if using.

Cook's tip

Cut a tiny slice from across the base of each peach or nectarine half, so that they sit steadily on the baking sheet.

Speedy Chocolate Sponge Puddings

Ⓥ

Time 20 minutes. Per portion: 655 Kcal, 40g fat (23.8g saturated)

Serves 4

Unsalted butter 150g (5oz), softened, plus a little extra for greasing

Caster sugar 110g (4oz) plus 2 tsp

Self-raising flour 110g (4oz)

Baking powder ¼ tsp

Cocoa 2 tbsp

Egg 1 large

Vanilla extract 1 tsp

Dark chocolate 110g (4oz), broken into small pieces

Milk 3 tbsp

Vanilla ice cream to serve (optional)

Scan the **QR Code** with a smartphone for an ingredients shopping list

Thoroughly grease individual pudding basins or microwave-suitable teacups with butter.

Place 110g (4oz) of butter and 110g (4oz) of caster sugar in a mixing bowl, sift the flour, baking powder and cocoa into the bowl, then add the egg, vanilla and 2 tablespoons of water. With an electric hand-held mixer, whisk the ingredients together until smooth.

Divide the chocolate mixture evenly between the pudding basins or teacups, loosely cover with cling film and microwave on high for 4 - 5 minutes, until the sponge is well risen and springy to the touch. Remove from the microwave and allow to stand while making the sauce.

To make the sauce: Put the chocolate in a small bowl with the 2 tsp sugar, the remaining butter and the milk. Place over a saucepan of gently simmering water and stir until smooth.

Run a palette knife around each pudding to loosen, trim the tops level if necessary, then turn the puddings out onto individual plates and coat with the chocolate sauce. Serve with ice cream, if you like.

Cook's tip

For marmalade puddings, omit the cocoa and vanilla and replace with the zest and juice from 1 orange. Spoon 50g (2oz) marmalade into each cup or basin before adding the sponge mixture. There's no need to make the sauce, simply serve with custard.

Rich and chocolatey, these individual puddings
cook in just a few minutes in the microwave,
giving you a midweek chocolate fix!

A delicious accompaniment to your favourite cheese and, as they're made from oats, they keep you full for longer.

Scottish Oatcakes

Time 30 minutes. Per oatcake: 59 Kcal, 2.9g fat (1.1g saturated)

Makes 12

Medium oatmeal 110g (4oz), plus extra for sprinkling

Salt ¼ tsp

Bicarbonate of soda ¼ tsp

Lard 25g (1oz)

Boiling water 2–3 tbsp

Scan the **QR Code** with a smartphone for an ingredients shopping list

Preheat the oven to 180°C/350°F/Gas 4 and grease a baking sheet. Put the oatmeal, salt and bicarbonate of soda into a bowl.

In a small saucepan, gently heat the lard until it has melted. Quickly pour enough of the liquid into the dry ingredients with the water to make a smooth dough.

Sprinkle some oatmeal onto a surface and roll out the dough to about 3mm (⅛in) thick. Then, using a 7.5cm (3in) round cutter, cut out 12 circles, re-rolling the dough if necessary.

Place the oatcakes on the baking sheet and cook in the oven for about 20 minutes until crisp. Serve lightly buttered with cheese, jam or honey.

Cook's tip

For a less coarse textured oatcake use fine oatmeal. Oatcakes can be stored in a sealed container in the cupboard for a couple of weeks. You can also freeze some if you need to keep them for longer.

Shrewsbury Biscuits

V

Time 30 minutes. Per biscuit: 104 Kcal, 4g fat (2.5g saturated)

Makes 24

Butter 110g (4oz)

Caster sugar 150g (5oz), plus extra for sprinkling

Egg yolks 2

Plain flour 225g (8oz)

Lemon 1, finely grated zest

Chopped dried fruit 50g (2oz)

Scan the **QR Code** with a smartphone for an ingredients shopping list

Preheat the oven to 180°C/350°F/Gas 4 and butter two non-stick baking sheets.

Cream the butter and sugar until pale and fluffy and add the egg yolks and beat well. Add the flour, lemon zest and fruit and mix to a fairly firm dough.

On a lightly floured surface, knead lightly and then roll out to about 5mm (¼in) thick. Cut out 6.5cm (2½in) circles with a round cutter and place on the baking sheets. Sprinkle with a little extra caster sugar.

Bake for 12–15 minutes until lightly browned and firm to the touch. Transfer to wire racks to cool. Store in an airtight container.

Cook's tip

If you enjoy spiced biscuits, omit the lemon zest and add 1 tsp mixed spice and 1 tsp cinnamon instead.

These classic biscuits simply melt
in the mouth. Choose any dried
fruit that you have in your cupboard.

Indulge your inner child with these soft
and scrummy cookies – a winner with
every member of the family.

Rocky Road Cookies

V F

Time 25 minutes. Per cookie: 221 Kcal, 10g fat (6g saturated)

Makes 10-12

Butter 110g (4oz), softened

Light muscovado sugar 110g (4oz)

Egg 1, beaten

Plain flour 150g (5oz)

Baking powder ½ tsp

Oats 75g (3oz)

Mini marshmallows 50g (2oz)

Plain chocolate 75g (3oz), chopped

Scan the **QR Code** with a smartphone for an ingredients shopping list

Preheat the oven to 180°C/350°F/Gas 4. Line a baking tray with non-stick baking paper.

In a large bowl, beat together the butter and sugar until light and creamy. Gradually beat in the egg.

Sift in the flour and baking powder and add the oats. Stir well. Add half the mini marshmallows and half the chopped chocolate.

Drop heaped tablespoonfuls of the mixture onto the prepared baking tray and bake for 10-15 minutes, until just turning golden. Sprinkle over the remaining marshmallows and chocolate chunks as soon as the cookies are removed from the oven. Leave to cool slightly, then transfer to a wire rack to cool completely.

Cook's tips

Swap marshmallows for dried fruit if you like. Sprinkle any leftover marshmallows over ice cream with a drizzle of golden syrup for a naughty dessert.

Oaty Apple & Banana Bars

V **F**

Time 30 minutes. Per portion: 160 Kcal, 8g fat (4.5g saturated)

Makes 18

Butter 150g (5oz)

Cooking apple 225g (8oz), peeled, cored and grated

Soft light brown sugar 150g (5oz)

Porridge oats 225g (8oz)

Banana chips 50g (2oz), broken into small pieces

Scan the **QR Code** with a smartphone for an ingredients shopping list

Preheat the oven to 190°C/375°F/Gas 5. Grease and base line a small 18 x 28 x 4cm (7 x 11 x 1½in) roasting tin with non-stick baking paper.

Melt the butter in a saucepan, add the apple and fry gently for 1-2 minutes until softened.

Add the sugar, oats and banana chips and stir well. Spoon the mixture into the tin and press flat. Cook for 20 minutes until golden brown, then take out of the oven, mark into bars and leave to cool completely.

Remove the slab from the tin, peel off the paper and cut into the marked bars.

Cook's tip

Banana chips are available from health food shops. If you can't find them, the recipe works just as well without.

Perfectly portable, these soft and scrummy oat bars are ideal for packing with a flask to keep those hunger pangs at bay while on the go.

This is a great dessert for entertaining as it looks
so pretty but can be made in advance – leaving
you time to spend with your guests.

Cherry Yogurt Ice

Ⓥ Ⓕ

Time 10 minutes plus freezing. Per portion: 146 Kcal, 2g fat (0.9g saturated)

Serves 8

Vanilla yogurt 2 x 450g tubs

Milk 6 tbsp

Caster sugar 25g (1oz)

Cherries 225g (8oz), halved and stoned

Scan the **QR Code** with a smartphone for an ingredients shopping list

Pour one tub of yogurt into a large plastic container. Whisk in the milk and sugar and then whisk in the other pot of yogurt. Put on the lid and freeze for 3 hours until almost solid.

Break up the frozen yogurt and then whisk well until almost smooth. Stir in the prepared cherries and then return to the freezer for 3 hours until firm. Take the ice cream out of the freezer 10 minutes before serving.

Cook's tips

If you have an ice cream maker, put the yogurt mixture in and follow the manufacturer's instructions, adding the cherries towards the end of the process. This recipe is perfect for cherry season when the fruits are plentiful. You can also make it with raspberries, strawberries or blueberries.

Syllabub Trifle

(V)

Time 20 minutes plus chilling. Per portion: 395 Kcal, 27g fat (15.1g saturated)

Serves 6

Trifle sponges 4

Raspberry jam 110g (4oz)

Lemon 1, grated zest and juice

Caster sugar 50g (2oz)

Dry cider with elderflower 120ml (4fl oz)

Double cream 300ml carton

Mixed frozen fruits 200g (7oz), just defrosted

Scan the **QR Code** with a smartphone for an ingredients shopping list

Slice each sponge cake in half horizontally. Spread jam over half of the slices, then cover with the remaining slices, cut to fit and place in six individual glasses in a single layer. Spread any remaining jam over the top of the sponge cakes.

Place most of the lemon zest, the lemon juice and sugar in a bowl. Add the cider and stir until the sugar has dissolved. Drizzle a little of this liquid over the trifle sponges until just moist.

Whip the cream until it forms soft peaks. Gradually whisk in the remaining cider mixture.

Spoon the fruit over the sponge and then cover with the flavoured cream. Top with any remaining lemon zest. Chill for 1-2 hours before serving.

Cook's tips

Use ordinary dry cider in place of the cider with elderflower if you wish. You could also try a fruity berry cider. You can use any type of jam that you have in your fridge.

This tangy twist on traditional trifle
tantalises the tastebuds!

You only need three ingredients to make this sweet and succulent winter dessert.

Caramel Clementines
with Rosemary

(V)

Time 30 minutes plus cooling. Per portion: 284 Kcal, 0g fat (0g saturated)

Serves 4

Clementines 8

Rosemary 2 sprigs, plus extra to decorate

Granulated sugar 250g (9oz)

Greek-style plain yogurt to serve (optional)

Scan the **QR Code** with a smartphone for an ingredients shopping list

Peel the clementines carefully so that they remain whole, then put them into a heatproof bowl with the rosemary sprigs.

Pour 250ml (8fl oz) water into a saucepan, add the sugar and heat gently, stirring very occasionally until the sugar has completely dissolved.

Increase the heat and boil the syrup for 8–10 minutes, without stirring, until it begins to turn pale golden. Keep a watchful eye towards the end of cooking as the syrup will suddenly begin to colour around the edges.

When the syrup has become gold all over, take the pan off the heat and add 6 tbsp boiling water (standing well back as the syrup may spit), then tilt the pan to mix. Once the bubbles have subsided, pour the hot syrup over the clementines and leave to cool for 2–3 hours.

Turn the clementines in the syrup, then transfer to a serving bowl. Discard the soaked rosemary and decorate with fresh. Serve with spoonfuls of Greek yogurt if you like.

Cook's tips

If you haven't made caramel syrup before, the secret is not to stir the syrup once it is boiling or the sugar will crystallise. If this happens, throw it away and start again. If you don't have rosemary, then add 3 star anise or try 2 tbsp of chopped glacé ginger instead.

Baked Apples

Time 45 minutes. Per portion: 223 Kcal, 8g fat (5.2g saturated)

Serves 4

Butter 40g (1½oz), softened

Light muscovado sugar 40g (1½oz)

Chopped glacé ginger 1 tbsp

Glacé cherries 25g (1oz), chopped

Ready-to-eat prunes 75g (3oz), chopped

Dessert apples 4

Custard to serve (optional)

Scan the **QR Code** with a smartphone for an ingredients shopping list

Preheat the oven to 180°C/350°F/Gas 4. Beat the butter and sugar together in a bowl until soft and smooth. Stir in the glacé ginger and then add the cherries and prunes.

Cut a thin slice off the top of each apple and reserve. Core the apples and cut a very thin slice off the bottom if needed, to stop them rolling around.

Stand the cored apples in a small 20cm (8in) circular dish, then press the fruit mixture into the cavities, spooning the remainder over the cut top edge. Press the apple lids back in place.

Add 2 tbsp of water to the base of the dish, then bake for 30 minutes until the apples are tender. Serve hot with custard, if you like.

Cook's tips

Dates and dried cranberries with a little ground cinnamon also work well in this recipe, or if you have some leftover Christmas mincemeat, add this. Glacé ginger can be found next to the glacé cherries in the supermarket. If you are unable to obtain it use ½ tsp ground ginger instead.

Soft, slightly sharp and stuffed with
ginger-infused fruit, these apples
are little parcels of deliciousness.

Meringue is always a popular choice and
topped with sweet, spiced plums, the
combination of textures is wonderful.

Coconut & Plum Pavlovas

(V)

Time 2 hours. Per portion: 526 Kcal, 35g fat (22.2g saturated)

Serves 6

Egg whites 3

Caster sugar 225g (8oz)

Cornflour 1 tsp

White wine vinegar 1 tsp

Desiccated coconut 75g (3oz)

Plums 450g (1lb), stoned and thickly sliced

Ground cinnamon ¼ tsp

Double cream 300ml pot

Plain yogurt 150g pot

Scan the **QR Code** with a smartphone for an ingredients shopping list

Preheat the oven to 110°C/225°F/Gas ¼. Line a large baking sheet with a sheet of non-stick baking paper. Whisk the egg whites in a large bowl with a hand-held electric mixer until they are stiff and the bowl can be turned upside down without the meringue moving.

Gradually whisk in 175g (6oz) sugar, a teaspoonful at a time and continue to whisk for 1–2 minutes until the meringue is very thick and glossy. Mix the cornflour and vinegar together, then fold into the meringue. Sprinkle the coconut over the top and fold in gently.

Spoon six large mounds of meringue onto the prepared baking sheet and spread them into swirly circles, each about 10cm (4in) in diameter. Bake the meringues for 1¼–1½ hours until the Pavlovas can be lifted off the paper easily. Set aside to cool.

Meanwhile, to make the topping, put the plums, remaining sugar and cinnamon together with 2 tablespoons of water into a saucepan. Simmer gently for 5–8 minutes until just tender but the fruit is still holding its shape, then leave to cool.

To serve, transfer the Pavlovas to serving plates. Whisk the cream in a bowl until it forms soft swirls then fold in the yogurt. Spoon the creamy mixture over the top of the Pavlovas and top with the plums.

Cook's tips

Use the leftover egg yolks in the Rich Lemon Chicken on page 66. Otherwise use to make proper custard. You could use damsons or rhubarb instead of plums if you prefer.

Brown Sugar Meringues
with Cinnamon Cream

(V)

Time 1½ hours. Per portion: 121 Kcal, 8g fat (4.5g saturated)

Makes 10 pairs

Egg whites 2

Light muscovado sugar
65g (2½oz)

Caster sugar 50g (2oz)

Double cream 150ml pot

Ground cinnamon ¼ tsp

Dark chocolate 50g (2oz),
chopped (optional)

Scan the **QR Code** with
a smartphone for an
ingredients shopping list

Preheat the oven to 110°C/225°F/Gas ¼. Line a large baking sheet with a sheet of non-stick baking paper. Whisk the egg whites in a large bowl with a hand-held electric mixer until they are stiff and the bowl can be turned upside down without the meringue moving.

Mix 50g (2oz) of the muscovado sugar with the caster sugar in a bowl then gradually whisk into the egg whites, a teaspoonful at a time and continue to whisk for 1–2 minutes until it is very thick and glossy.

Using a dessertspoon, take a scoop of meringue, slide the bowl of a second dessertspoon into the first spoon to shape the meringue into a neat oval. Slide it off the second spoon with the help of the first spoon on to the paper. Continue until all the meringue has been shaped and you have about 20 meringues.

Bake the meringues for 1–1¼ hours or until they can be lifted off the paper easily. Leave to cool.

To serve, pour the cream into a bowl, add the remaining sugar and cinnamon and whisk until it forms soft swirls, then use it to sandwich the meringues together. Place them in paper cases.

If using the chocolate, place in a heatproof bowl over a barely simmering saucepan of water and stir until it has melted. Drizzle over the meringues.

Cook's tip

The cooled, unfilled meringues can be packed into a biscuit tin lined with non-stick baking paper and will keep for up to 1 week.

These little delicacies are so pretty they make a stunning centrepiece. Simply stack on a dainty glass dish.

A comforting pudding made with a mix of red plums, apples and blackberries picked from the hedgerow, topped with a light orange sponge.

Orchard Sponge Pudding

Time 1 hour. Per portion: 368 Kcal, 12g fat (6.9g saturated)

Serves 4

Plums 250g (9oz), stoned and thickly sliced

Cooking apples 450g (1lb), cored, peeled and sliced

Blackberries 150g (5oz)

Caster sugar 110g (4oz)

Small orange 1, grated zest and juice

Butter 50g (2oz)

Self-raising flour 75g (3oz)

Egg 1

Sifted icing sugar to decorate (optional)

Custard to serve (optional)

Scan the **QR Code** with a smartphone for an ingredients shopping list

Preheat the oven to 180°C/350°F/Gas 4. Put the sliced plums, apples and blackberries into a 1.2 litre (2 pint) ovenproof pie dish. Sprinkle over half the sugar and half the orange juice and then bake for 10 minutes.

Put the remaining sugar with the orange zest, butter, flour and egg into a bowl and beat together with a hand-held electric mixer or wooden spoon until smooth. Gradually beat in the remaining orange juice, being careful not to over mix or the topping may split.

Flatten the partially cooked fruit slightly with the back of a spoon, then spoon the sponge mixture over the top and spread into an even layer. Bake for 25-30 minutes until the topping is well risen and golden and springs back when pressed with a fingertip. Dust with icing sugar and serve warm with custard, if using.

Cook's tip

A mixture of fresh fruit has been used here, but you could use some frozen fruits or 850g (1lb 14oz) of just one kind of fruit if preferred.

Sticky Toffee & Banana Pudding

V **F**

Time 1 hour. Per portion: 540 Kcal, 16g fat (9.3g saturated)

Serves 6

Pitted dates 175g (6oz), chopped

Bicarbonate of soda 1 tsp

Butter 110g (4oz), softened, plus a little extra for greasing

Caster sugar 175g (6oz)

Self-raising flour 175g (6oz)

Eggs 2

Vanilla extract 1 tsp

Golden syrup 4 tbsp

Light muscovado sugar 4 tbsp

Ripe bananas 2, peeled and halved lengthways

Lemon ½, juice only

Vanilla ice cream to serve (optional)

Scan the **QR Code** with a smartphone for an ingredients shopping list

Preheat the oven to 180°C/350°F/Gas 4. Place the dates and 300ml (½ pint) of water in a small saucepan and simmer for 10 minutes until the dates are soft. Take off the heat and stir in the bicarbonate of soda.

Butter a 20cm (8in) square 5cm (2in) deep ovenproof dish then line the base with a piece of greaseproof or non-stick baking paper.

With a hand-held electric mixer beat 50g (2oz) butter in a bowl with the caster sugar, flour, eggs and vanilla extract until smooth, then stir in the dates and liquid.

Spoon the golden syrup into the base of the dish, then sprinkle with the muscovado sugar and remaining butter, diced. Toss the bananas in the lemon juice. Arrange, cut-side down, in the dish, spoon the date mixture over the top and level the surface. Bake for about 35 minutes until well risen and the centre springs back when pressed with a fingertip.

To turn out, loosen the edges of the pudding with a knife, cover with a large plate and invert on to the plate, holding the dish with a teacloth. Remove the dish, peel off the lining paper and cut the pudding into pieces. Serve with scoops of ice cream, if using.

Cook's tip

You needn't wait for your bananas at home to ripen sufficiently for this dish; discounted overly ripe bananas are often available.

Who could resist this winning combo of syrupy banoffee pudding perfection?

Crumble with a twist: the almond flavour of grated marzipan in the topping complements the plums beneath perfectly.

Plum & Marzipan Crumble

Time 40 minutes. Per portion: 334 Kcal, 13g fat (7.3g saturated)

Serves 8

Plums 900g (2lb), halved and stoned

Caster sugar 175g (6oz)

Plain flour 225g (8oz)

Butter 110g (4oz), cubed

Marzipan 110g (4oz), coarsely grated

Vanilla ice cream to serve (optional)

Scan the **QR Code** with a smartphone for an ingredients shopping list

Preheat the oven to 190°C/375°F/Gas 5.

Put the plums into a saucepan with 110g (4oz) sugar and 3 tbsp water. Cook, uncovered, for about 10 minutes until the plums are just tender.

To make the topping, put the flour into a bowl with the remaining sugar. Add the butter and rub it in with your fingertips until the mixture resembles fine breadcrumbs, then stir in the marzipan.

Pour the plums into an ovenproof dish and spoon the crumble over the top. Place in the oven and cook for about 20 minutes until the topping is golden. Serve hot with vanilla ice cream, if using.

Cook's tips

Vary the fruits according to the season; cooking apples, rhubarb and gooseberries all work well. Any leftover marzipan can be used to top cakes or pop inside croissants (you can buy ready-to-bake croissant dough in a can). Omit the marzipan from the topping if you are not keen.

Marmalade Bread & Butter Pudding

V F

Time 45 minutes. Per portion: 574 Kcal, 25g fat (13g saturated)

Serves 2

White bread 6 slices, crusts removed

Butter 40g (1½oz), softened

Marmalade 2 tbsp

Caster sugar 2 tbsp

Sultanas 2 tbsp

Eggs 2

Milk 200ml (7fl oz)

Scan the **QR Code** with a smartphone for an ingredients shopping list

Preheat the oven to 190°C/375°F/Gas 5 and lightly butter a 600ml (1 pint) pie dish.

Spread the bread with butter and then with the marmalade and then cut each slice of bread into four triangles. Arrange the triangles in the prepared dish, sprinkling the layers with sugar and sultanas.

Beat the eggs and milk together in a jug, then pour into the dish. Bake in the oven for about 30 minutes until golden brown and set. Serve warm.

Cook's tips

Choose a rough-cut marmalade for added texture, or try lime marmalade, for a change. Try using other chopped dried fruits instead of sultanas.

This British classic with the addition of marmalade for bitter-sweet flavour is perfect for using up stale bread.

This pretty pudding is fantastic for making use of a glut of home-grown gooseberries. It's equally good served hot or cold, but it won't last long!

Gooseberry & Almond Tart

V **F**

Time 50 minutes. Per portion: 424 Kcal, 28g fat (9.1g saturated)

Serves 8

Dessert shortcrust pastry
375g pack, thawed if frozen

Butter 50g (2oz)

Caster sugar 110g (4oz)

Ground almonds 100g pack

Eggs 1 whole plus 1 egg yolk

Gooseberries 250g (9oz)

Icing sugar for dusting
(optional)

**Crème fraîche or double
cream** to serve (optional)

Scan the **QR Code** with
a smartphone for an
ingredients shopping list

Roll out the pastry on a lightly floured surface until a little larger than a 23cm (9in) diameter fluted loose-based flan tin. Lift the pastry over the rolling pin, and into the tin then ease up the sides, pressing it in place with your fingertips. Trim the top of the pastry so that it stands a little above the top of the tin. You will have pastry left over to make some jam tarts.

Preheat the oven to 200°C/400°F/Gas 6. Chill the pastry case while the oven heats up, or longer if you have the time.

To make the filling, melt the butter in a large bowl (in the microwave or over a pan of simmering water). Add all but 1 tablespoon of the sugar and beat well. Stir in the ground almonds, egg and egg yolk, then spoon the mixture into the flan case.

Put the gooseberries on top and sprinkle with the remaining sugar. Bake in the bottom half of the oven, which should help prevent a soggy-bottomed tart, for 30–35 minutes until the filling is firm and golden brown. Serve warm or at room temperature dusted with icing sugar and a spoonful of crème fraîche or double cream, if using.

Cook's tips

If you have lots of gooseberries, bag them and freeze. To make tarts with any leftover pastry, stamp out circles with a cutter, fill with a heaped teaspoon of jam or mincemeat and bake for 10-12 minutes until the pastry is golden.

Treacle Tart with Glazed Apples

Ⓥ Ⓕ

Time 1¼ hours plus cooling. Per portion: 555 Kcal, 16g fat (7.2g saturated)

Serves 6

Plain flour 175g (6oz)

Butter 65g (2½oz), diced

White vegetable cooking fat or lard 40g (1½oz), diced

Golden syrup 454g tin

Ground ginger 1 tsp

Lemon 1, grated zest and juice

Fresh breadcrumbs 110g (4oz)

Cooking apples 2, peeled, cored and thinly sliced

Icing sugar 1 tbsp

Custard or ice cream to serve (optional)

Scan the **QR Code** with a smartphone for an ingredients shopping list

To make the pastry, put the flour, 40g (1½oz) butter and fat in a bowl and rub in with your fingertips until you have fine crumbs. Gradually add 2 tbsp water and mix to a smooth dough. Alternatively, you could use a food processor.

Knead the pastry briefly, then roll out on a lightly floured surface until a little larger than a 24cm (9½in) diameter fluted loose-bottomed flan tin. Lift the pastry over the rolling pin, place in the tin then ease up the sides, pressing it in place. Trim the top of the pastry so that it stands a little above the tin. Chill for 15 minutes.

Meanwhile, preheat the oven to 190°C/375°F/Gas 5. Pour the syrup into a saucepan, add the ginger, lemon zest and half the juice and gently heat. Take the pan off the heat and stir in the breadcrumbs. Leave to cool.

Pour the syrup into the tart case. Toss the apple in the remaining lemon juice. Arrange the slices, overlapping, in rings over the top of the tart. Then melt the remaining butter and brush it over the apples. Bake for about 35 minutes until the apples are golden.

Sift the icing sugar over the top and return the tart to the oven for a further 5 minutes or until the sugar has caramelised. Leave to cool for 30 minutes, then remove the tart from the tin and cut into wedges. Serve with ice cream or custard, if you like.

Cook's tip

Place any stale bread you have in a food procssor and whizz into breadcrumbs. Separate into portions and freeze in polythene bags so that you have a ready-made supply.

This old-fashioned favourite gets the French treatment by topping it with thinly sliced cooking apples. It looks simply stunning.

We've all been guilty of buying too many bananas and then forgetting to eat them when at their best. Don't consign them to the bin, use them in this homely cherry cake.

Cherry, Pineapple & Banana Cake

V **F**

Time 1½ hours. Per portion: 305 Kcal, 10g fat (6.1g saturated)

Makes 10 slices

Self-raising flour 225g (8oz)

Butter 110g (4oz), diced

Caster sugar 150g (5oz)

Eggs 2

Ripe bananas 450g (1lb), weighed in their skins

Glacé cherries 150g (5oz)

Pineapple chunks 227g can, drained and chopped

Few sugar lumps roughly crushed to decorate (optional)

Scan the **QR Code** with a smartphone for an ingredients shopping list

Preheat the oven to 160°C/325°F/Gas 3. Grease an 18cm (7in) deep round cake tin and line the base with a circle of greaseproof or non-stick baking paper.

Put the flour and butter into a bowl and rub in with your fingertips until the mixture resembles fine breadcrumbs. Stir in the sugar and then beat in the eggs one at a time.

Peel the bananas and mash on a plate with a fork then beat into the cake mixture. Halve 8 of the cherries and reserve for decoration, then cut the rest into quarters and add these to the cake mixture with the drained pineapple pieces. Gently stir the cake until just mixed then spoon into the prepared tin.

Spread the top level and decorate with a ring of the reserved cherry halves and a few crushed sugar lumps, if using. Bake the cake for 1–1¼ hours or until the top is golden and slightly cracked and a skewer comes out cleanly when inserted into the centre.

Leave the cake to cool in the tin for 15 minutes, then loosen the edges with a knife and turn out on to a wire rack. Leave to cool before peeling off the lining paper. Store in an airtight tin for up to 1 week.

Cook's tips

If you have some sugar lumps at the back of the cupboard, then break up a few with a rolling pin and use to decorate the cake. If not, simply leave them out. Any leftover cherries can be used to top fairy cakes.

Chocolate & Coffee Cake

(V) (F)

Time 50 minutes. Per portion: 475 Kcal, 27.4g fat (16.4g saturated)

Makes 8–10 slices

Butter 300g (11oz)

Light muscovado sugar 175g (6oz)

Self-raising flour 150g (5oz)

Cocoa powder 25g (1oz)

Baking powder 1 tsp

Eggs 3

Instant coffee 2 tsp

Icing sugar 250g (9oz)

Dark chocolate 25g (1oz) (optional), grated

Scan the **QR Code** with a smartphone for an ingredients shopping list

Preheat the oven to 180°C/350°F/Gas 4. Lightly oil two 18cm (7in) diameter victoria sandwich tins and line the base of each with a circle of greaseproof or non-stick baking paper.

Put 175g (6oz) butter, the muscovado sugar, flour, cocoa, baking powder and eggs into a mixing bowl or food processor bowl and beat together until smooth. Divide between the cake tins and smooth the surface with a round-bladed knife.

Bake for 20 minutes until the cakes are well risen and, when pressed in the centre lightly with a fingertip, the cake springs back. Cool for 5 minutes then loosen the edges of the cakes with a knife, turn out onto a wire rack, peel off the lining paper and leave to cool.

Meanwhile, make the filling by mixing the instant coffee and 1 tsp boiling water together until smooth. Add the remaining butter to a mixing bowl or food processor bowl with half the icing sugar and beat until light and fluffy. Add the remaining sugar and cooled coffee and beat once more until smooth.

Transfer one of the cakes to a serving plate, spoon half the butter icing on top and spread into an even layer. Add the second cake and spread the remaining icing on top. Sprinkle with grated chocolate, if using.

Cook's tip

Use leftover cocoa powder and dark chocolate to make decadent hot chocolate:
Put 1 tbsp of cocoa powder and 2 tbsp of sugar into a mug with 1 tbsp of grated chocolate.
Pour on hot milk and stir.

Meeting friends in a café can be expensive,
so why not host at home? It's more relaxed
and you get to show off your baking skills.

Packed full of fruit, this moist teabread is almost fat-free and makes the perfect snack.

Mixed Fruit Teabread

Ⓥ Ⓕ

Time 1½ hours plus soaking. Per portion: 253 Kcal, 1g fat (0.2g saturated)

Makes 10 slices

Hot tea 300ml (½ pint)

Mixed dried fruit 300g (11oz)

Chopped mixed peel 2 tbsp (optional)

Dessert apple 1, cored but not peeled

Egg 1, beaten

Caster sugar 150g (5oz)

Self-raising flour 300g (11oz)

Ground mixed spice 1 tsp

Pumpkin seeds 2 tbsp (optional)

Scan the **QR Code** with a smartphone for an ingredients shopping list

Pour the hot tea into a large bowl, add the dried fruit and chopped mixed peel, if using, and leave to soak for 3 hours or overnight.

Preheat the oven to 160°C/325°F/Gas 3. Lightly oil a 900g (2lb) loaf tin and line the two long sides and base with a strip of greaseproof or non-stick baking paper.

Coarsely grate the apple into the soaked fruit and add the egg to the bowl with the sugar, flour and spice then stir together until smooth.

Pour the mixture into the prepared cake tin, spread level then sprinkle with the seeds, if using. Bake the cake for about 1¼ hours or until the top is slightly cracked and a skewer comes out cleanly when inserted into the centre.

Leave the cake to cool in the tin for 15 minutes, then loosen the edges with a knife and turn out onto a wire rack. Leave to cool before peeling off the lining paper. Serve thickly sliced and buttered.

Cook's tips

This cake stores well in a cake tin or plastic box for up to 1 week.
Any leftover fruit and seeds can be mixed with oats, apple
and yogurt to make delicious muesli.

Gooey Gingerbread

V F

Time 45 minutes. Per portion: 157 Kcal, 6g fat (3.5g saturated)

Makes 18 bars

Butter 110g (4oz)

Granulated sugar 75g (3oz)

Golden syrup 225g (8oz)

Marmalade 2 tbsp

Self-raising flour 225g (8oz)

Ground ginger 2 tsp

Bicarbonate of soda ½ tsp

Milk 150ml (¼ pint)

Eggs 2

Scan the **QR Code** with
a smartphone for an
ingredients shopping list

Preheat the oven to 180°C/350°F/Gas 4. Butter a small roasting tin measuring about 18 x 28 x 4cm (7 x 11 x 1½in) and base line with non-stick baking paper.

Put the butter, sugar, syrup and marmalade into a saucepan and heat, stirring, until the butter has melted and the sugar dissolved. Take the pan off the heat and leave to cool slightly.

Mix the flour, ginger and bicarbonate of soda together in a bowl, then stir into the cooled butter and sugar mixture.

Beat the milk and eggs together, then stir into the ginger mixture. Pour into the prepared tin, level the surface and cook for about 25 minutes until the cake is well risen and golden. The cake is ready when the top springs back when pressed with your fingertips.

Leave the cake to cool in the tin, then take it out of the tin, peel off the paper and cut it into bars.

Cook's tips

To store, wrap in foil and then keep in an airtight tub or tin.
It's also delicious as a pudding with a splash of hot custard.

The best kind of gingerbread is the sticky variety – you won't find this particular cake hanging around for long as it's much better than anything shop-bought.

Warm, buttery Eccles cakes are just
perfect served with a hot pot of tea in
the company of good friends.

Luxury Eccles Cakes

Ⓥ Ⓕ

Time 40 minutes. Per portion: 223 Kcal, 13g fat (5.7g saturated)
Makes 12

Luxury mixed dried fruits
175g (6oz)

Dark muscovado sugar 50g
(2oz)

Ground mixed spice 1 tsp

Grated nutmeg ½ tsp

Lemon 1, finely grated zest only

Butter 40g (1½oz), melted

Ready-rolled puff pastry 375g
packet

Egg 1, beaten

Caster sugar for sifting

Scan the **QR Code** with
a smartphone for an
ingredients shopping list

Preheat the oven to 220°C/425°F/Gas 7 and grease
two baking sheets. In a large bowl, mix together the
dried fruits, sugar, spices, lemon zest and the butter.

Lay the pastry on a lightly floured surface and using a
9cm (3½in) plain round cutter, stamp as many rounds
as you can from the pastry and set aside.

Re-fold the pastry trimmings, in layers, and then
re-roll and stamp out more rounds until you have 12
of them.

Dividing evenly, place a rounded teaspoonful of
the fruit mixture in the centre of each pastry circle.
Brush the edges with cold water, then bring the sides
of the pastry up and over the filling and pinch firmly
together to seal. Turn over and gently flatten with your
hand.

Place the Eccles cakes on the greased baking trays
and brush lightly with beaten egg, then lightly score
the tops, diagonally, three times. Bake for 12–15
minutes until the cakes are well risen, golden brown
and crisp to the touch.

Sift the Eccles cakes with caster sugar while they are
still hot. Eat warm, or leave until cold.

Cook's tips

Eccles cakes stored in an airtight tin will keep well for several days.
You can use raisins in place of the luxury dried fruits if you prefer.

Chocolate Brownies

Time 55 minutes. Per portion: 122 Kcal, 4g fat (1.6g saturated)

Makes 16

Prunes in fruit juice 410g can

Eggs 2

Caster sugar 110g (4oz)

Cocoa powder 50g (2oz)

Plain flour 50g (2oz)

Baking powder 1 tsp

Cook's dark chocolate 75g (3oz)

Scan the **QR Code** with a smartphone for an ingredients shopping list

Preheat the oven to 180°C/350°F/Gas 4. Line an 18cm (7in) shallow square tin with greaseproof or non-stick baking paper. Snip the paper at the corners, press it into the tin and secure the corners with paper clips.

Drain the prunes, remove the stones and put the fruit into a liquidiser or food processor. Blend to a purée.

In a bowl, whisk the eggs and sugar until they are pale and frothy and the whisk leaves a trail of mixture when lifted above the bowl.

Fold in the prune purée, then sift in the cocoa, flour and baking powder and carefully fold in.

Pour the mixture into the prepared tin and tilt to level the mixture. Cook for 30-35 minutes until the cake is well risen and a skewer comes out cleanly when inserted into the centre. Leave the cake to cool in the tin.

Meanwhile, break the chocolate into pieces and place in a heatproof bowl. Stand the bowl over a barely simmering saucepan of water, ensuring the bottom of the bowl doesn't touch the water. Melt the chocolate, then spoon it over the cake and spread in a thin layer. Leave to set.

Lift the cake out of the tin, peel off the paper and cut into 16 squares.

Cook's tips

Once cut, individually wrap a few brownies, then freeze. When unexpected visitors arrive simply unwrap and heat in the microwave for a few seconds. You can use milk chocolate in place of the dark chocolate if you prefer.

So soft and succulent, these melt-in-the-mouth
brownies will wow your friends and family.

These pretty little snowballs taste
scrumptious and are a firm favourite
with children and adults alike.

Snowballs

V **F**

Time 1 hour plus setting. Per portion: 173 Kcal, 7g fat (5.1g saturated)

Makes 16

Plain flour 110g (4oz)

Self-raising flour 110g (4oz)

Salt ½ tsp

Caster sugar 75g (3oz)

Unsalted butter 75g (3oz), cubed

Eggs 1 whole plus 1 egg yolk

Icing sugar 150g (5oz)

Vanilla extract a few drops

Desiccated coconut 75g (3oz)

Scan the **QR Code** with a smartphone for an ingredients shopping list

Preheat the oven to 200°C/400°F/Gas 6 and lightly grease a baking sheet.

Sift the flours and salt into a bowl and stir in the caster sugar. Rub in the butter until the mixture resembles fine breadcrumbs and bind together with the egg and egg yolk to form a firm dough.

Turn onto a lightly floured surface and knead very gently until smooth. Cut into four equal pieces, and then cut each piece into four. Roll each portion into a small ball and place on the prepared baking sheet.

Bake in the oven for about 15 minutes until golden and firm. Transfer to a wire rack to cool completely.

Sift 50g (2oz) of the icing sugar into a bowl then bind together with a little vanilla extract and sufficient water – about 1½ tsp – to form a stiff icing. Sandwich two cakes together from the flat sides with the icing to form small balls and then rest on a wire rack for about 30 minutes to set.

Sift the remaining icing sugar into a bowl, and add a few drops of the vanilla extract and 2 tbsp of water and mix to make a thinner, brushable icing. Brush the cakes all over with the icing and sprinkle with coconut. Place on a wire rack over a tray or plate to set for a further 30 minutes. Serve in cake cases.

Cook's tips

Add ½ teaspoon of finely grated lemon rind to the cake mixture for a citrusy flavour. You can freeze the snowballs before they are filled. They will keep for up to 3 months

Cherry & Pistachio Chocolate Squares

Ⓥ Ⓕ

Time 20 mins plus chilling. Per portion: 211 Kcal, 13g fat (6.6g saturated)

Makes 20

Butter 125g (4½oz), diced

Dark chocolate 300g (11oz), broken into squares

Golden syrup 3 tbsp

Glacé cherries 100g (3½oz), halved

Pistachio nuts 50g (2oz), chopped

Sultanas 50g (2oz)

Digestive biscuits 200g pack, broken into pieces

Scan the **QR Code** with a smartphone for an ingredients shopping list

Line a 20cm (8in) square tin with clingfilm.

Put the butter, chocolate and golden syrup into a large microwave-proof bowl. Microwave on medium power for 1-2 minutes until the chocolate has melted, stirring after every 20 seconds and checking the chocolate does not overheat.

Add the other ingredients and mix well. Spoon into the prepared tin and spread out evenly. Leave to cool.

Chill for at least an hour (or until set) and then remove from the tin, peel off the cling film and cut into 20 squares.

Cook's tips

Take care when melting the chocolate – if it is cooked for too long it will seize.
These squares will keep for a week wrapped in foil in the fridge or freeze for 3 months.
Use any dried fruits you have in the cupboard.

An easy, no bake recipe that's perfect to
make with children. It may be naughty,
but it's very very nice!

The price of bread has rocketed over the last few years, so why not make your own? A bowl of soup and a thick slice of homemade bread make a delicious supper.

Oat & Honey Bread

(V) (F)

Time 45 mins plus proving. Per portion: 182 Kcal, 3g fat (0.4g saturated)

Makes 1 loaf

Strong white flour 250g (9oz), plus extra for dusting

Wholemeal, granary or malthouse flour 250g (9oz)

Porridge oats 50g (2oz), plus extra for sprinkling

Salt ½ tsp

Set or runny honey 2 tbsp

Sunflower oil 2 tbsp

Easy blend dried yeast 2 tsp

Milk for glazing

Scan the **QR Code** with a smartphone for an ingredients shopping list

Stir together the flours, oats and salt in a large mixing bowl. Add the honey and oil then sprinkle the yeast over the top. Gradually mix in 300ml (½ pint) warm water until it forms a soft but not sticky dough, adjusting the amounts slightly if needed.

Turn the dough out onto a lightly floured surface and knead for 5 minutes until the dough feels soft and elastic. Lightly oil a 20cm (8in) diameter springform tin and press the dough into the centre so that it is flattened slightly but doesn't quite reach the sides.

Cover the dough loosely with oiled cling film and leave in a warm place to rise for 45–60 minutes until it is almost to the top of the tin. Towards the end of the proving time preheat the oven to 220°C/425°F/Gas 7.

Remove the cling film from the bread, brush the top lightly with a little milk then sprinkle with a few oats and a little flour. Bake for 30 minutes until well risen, browned and the top sounds hollow when tapped with your fingertips.

Loosen the edge of the bread with a round-bladed knife then remove from the tin and leave to cool on a wire rack.

Cook's tip

If you are not sure how warm the water should be when making bread, dip your little finger into the water. It should feel just warm at 37°C (98.4°F). Yeast needs warmth to activate it, but if the temperature is too hot – 54°C (130°F) or over – the yeast will be killed.

Thanks to

Executive Editor	Nick Rowe
Managing Editor	Emily Davenport
Designer	Graham Meigh
Editor	Emma Callery
Photographer	Steve Lee
Food Stylist	Sara Lewis
Props Stylist	Olivia Wardle

Recipes created by

Sara Lewis p10-171 except:
Pat Alburey p30, 130, 162
Kathryn Hawkins p18, 24, 40, 82, 110, 122, 150, 166, 168
Lucy Knox p116
Claire Lewis p80, 126
Sue McMahon p32, 46, 62, 64, 120
Kate Moseley p20, 26, 44, 48, 50, 54, 70, 72, 124

Proof Reader	Aune Butt
Indexer	Ruth Ellis
Nutritional Consultant	Wendy Doyle

Recipe Testers

Richard Davenport	Ann McClelland	Lucy Padget
Katy Hackforth	Penny Meigh	Christopher Perry
Diane Hopping	Claire Nadin	Laura Pickering

Production   Cath Linter

Eaglemoss Consumer Publications Ltd
Electra House, Electra Way, Crewe, Cheshire, CW1 6WZ
Telephone 01270 270050

Website www.dairydiary.co.uk

Blog www.dairydiarychat.co.uk

First printed May2014
© Eaglemoss Consumer Publications Ltd
ISBN: 978-0-9571772-2-2

123456789